Eavesdroppings

Bob Green

Eavesdroppings

Stories from Small Towns When Sin Was Fun

BOB GREEN

THE DUNDURN GROUP
TORONTO

Copy-editor: Michael Carroll
Design: Jennifer Scott
Printer: University of Toronto Press

Library and Archives Canada Cataloguing in Publication

Green, Bob, 1930-
      Eavesdroppings : stories from small towns when sin was fun / Bob Green.

Stories previously published in the Cambridge reporter.

ISBN-13: 978-1-55002-629-0
ISBN-10: 1-55002-629-1

      1. City and town life--Ontario--History--Humour. I. Title.
II. Title: Cambridge reporter.

PS8613.R42E29 2006   971.3'040207   C2006-902684-X

1   2   3   4   5   10   09   08   07   06

  Canada

We acknowledge the support of the **Canada Council for the Arts** and the **Ontario Arts Council** for our publishing program. We also acknowledge the financial support of the **Government of Canada** through the **Book Publishing Industry Development Program** and **The Association for the Export of Canadian Books**, and the **Government of Ontario** through the **Ontario Book Publishers Tax Credit program**, and the **Ontario Media Development Corporation**.

Printed and bound in Canada.
Printed on recycled paper.

www.dundurn.com

Dundurn Press	Gazelle Book Services Limited	Dundurn Press
3 Church Street, Suite 500	White Cross Mills	2250 Military Road
Toronto, Ontario, Canada	High Town, Lancaster, England	Tonawanda, NY
M5E 1M2	LA1 4XS	U.S.A. 14150

To Rufus and Morris,
who couldn't care less

Contents

Acknowledgements

Much gratitude to Robert Kerr and Graeme Ferguson, who dragged a neglected manuscript from my closet to be published for fun, glory, and mischief, and who knew where to take it. And thanks, too, to Anna Porter for liking the manuscript and giving advice and direction.

I would also like to thank Jane Burnside for typing the revisions again and again; Don Burnside for keeping the computer going; Bill Taylor, my landlord, for the hickory firewood that warmed my trailer; Iris Mitten for food, shelter, and laughs when I broke my ankle; and Rose Orth for wisdom and stability.

Preface

The preface — this thing — is the toughest part of a book to write because it has to account for what follows: the selection of personal experiences and the experiences of acquaintances, narrated without moral or political purpose, recalling, for fun more than anything else, the humorous side of solemn or outrageous events in the legends of small towns.

I've used the real names of all persons involved which, I trust, will lend the stories some historical credence.

Digressions, I must admit, became a problem. While trying to focus on local events, I wound up recounting the extraction of a beer glass from a man's rectum in the emergency ward of a Toronto hospital, and the flight of a Salvation Army bass drum through the show window of a gay bar in San Francisco. However, digressions of this sort are unavoidable when one considers what mathematicians tell us — that all people and the events they are involved in are at most only six degrees removed.

It's the small-world effect. We are all connected, and I assume that the stories related here, if pursued further, would connect us to similar events and people in every small town and city in North America.

Bob Green
Cambridge, Ontario
April 2006

1
The Great Airship

One August night in 1935 my mother said to me as she was putting me to bed, "I'll wake you early in the morning and get you dressed —" something she did for the next twenty years "— and we'll go outside for a big surprise."

Needless to say, she didn't have to wake me in the morning. I lay listening to the robins chirp at the sunrise. I heard Pop drive off to work at Scott Shoe before seven. Mom didn't give me a clue while we ate breakfast, but she kept looking out the window at the sky.

"A lot of little airplanes circling up there," she said. "They must be waiting for it."

It!

I was soon outside with Mom and sister Shirley looking up at the little planes, standing with all our neighbours in the middle of Lowrey Avenue in Galt, Ontario. Someone hollered, "Here it comes!" The buzz of little airplanes faded beneath the drum of heavier engines. Everyone turned towards the treetops to the west and gasped. An enormous silver airship the size of an ocean liner slid directly overhead. It was the *Graf Zeppelin*.

The famous German dirigible had been touring the United States, and this morning its flight from the Chicago World's Fair to Toronto's Canadian National Exhibition carried it right over our town. Sunlight glinted off its upper ridge and flickered off the long propeller blades of diesel engines slung below. A long gondola snug against the underside near the nose conveyed seventy notables of the Third Reich who peered down at us. I didn't know this at the time but read it years later.

When you are five, you totter in circles while staring up at the sky and tend to fall down. I remember doing this while holding on to my sister's hand. The zeppelin's huge tail fins stay in my mind. They were bright red and centred by white circles framing strange black hooked crosses. Swastikas. I didn't want the airship to pass. I couldn't see enough of it. But in two minutes it was gone, followed by the little airplanes. Then all was quiet and we stood and gazed at the empty sky for a long time.

Up on Highway 8, just north of the delta (Hunter's Corner), Helen Patterson of Preston rode in her father's car as he drove Aunt Jessie from Clyde to Kitchener to catch a train for Port Huron, Michigan, where she worked as a nurse. The zeppelin, a mile to the south, caught their eyes. They didn't know it was coming or even what it was. It was unworldly, and they had to stop to watch it pass. They forgot all about the train and missed it.

Strangely, few people here today remember this great spectacle. Even my sister, Shirley, forgot it, and until her memory revived I began to wonder if I might have simply dreamt it. However, Jim Rintoul remembered it, too, and phoned me.

The great zeppelin flew 590 flights, more than one million miles without a mishap, all the time captained by Dr. Hugo Ecker, then in his seventies. The airship was 776 feet long, 113 feet thick, and was held aloft by 3,945,720 cubic feet of hydrogen gas ... more than that released by our House of Commons during a Depression-year debate. Five 530-horsepower diesel engines enabled the ship to cruise at seventy miles per hour in still air. In 1936 the *Graf Zeppelin* was dismantled and replaced by the *Hindenburg*, which exploded at Lakehurst, New Jersey, in 1937.

A second *Graf Zeppelin* was built in 1938 and dispatched on a goodwill tour around the coastline of Britain. It was loaded with electronic gear to check out Britain's radar defence system. British spies learned of this and had the system turned off. British Prime Minister Neville Chamberlain hailed the goodwill tour as evidence of Adolf Hitler's peaceful intentions.

2
The Fascination of Main Street

The *Graf Zeppelin* was my first vivid memory. Subsequent memories, though not as spectacular, are just as precious.

On any Saturday night in downtown Galt back in the 1930s, automobiles bumper to bumper on Main Street between the unsynchronized traffic lights at Water and Ainslie chugged up such a din that jaywalkers had to shout to one another. And the sidewalks were so crowded that the fit and able walked on the pavement. Most people weren't out to shop but just to walk and talk, a luxury of the Great Depression. Patrons of *Gone with the Wind* lined two abreast from the Capitol Theatre on Water Street to the Imperial Bank at Main and around the corner to jostle with people pushing in and out of Walker Stores.

One Saturday afternoon near Christmas 1938, so many people jammed Walker's that the elevators couldn't handle them all and the stairs collapsed. Galt firemen mistook dust billowing from the windows to be smoke and turned on the hoses. Aside from a lot of shoppers soaked to the hide, the only serious casualty was a girl with a compound leg fracture.

Moviegoers lined up to the corner of Main were harangued by a street preacher from Hamilton who drew apocryphal omens on the road with coloured chalk. He raged against sex and violence and assorted vulgarities on the silver screen until his eyes bugged out and flecks of foam gathered on his moustache. When jeered, he raged against jeering. He raged against the Salvation Army Band (heretics he called them) gently huffing hymns at the corner of Main and Mill streets beside Rouse's Music Store, which sold radios, refrigerators, and washing machines.

Danny Oliver cruised the street, taking everything in. A spindly man always sporting a black bowler hat and a carnation in his lapel, Danny nervously marked time with his toed-up dusty black shoes and twitched his nose like a rabbit. Every few minutes he bolted away,

17

cursing at the top of his lungs, but soon sneaked back to mark time and twitch. Today we would say he had Tourette's syndrome.

Directly across from Walker Stores, Lee Bing's second-floor restaurant enclosed its patrons in muted green upholstered enclaves affording such privacy and quiet that diners in each cubicle peered out a lot to see who might be in the next. Bing McCauley, whose Bing is not to be confused with Lee's Bing, said that Lee once told him he had survived the sinking of the *Titanic*. He had been a steward but wouldn't discuss how he got off with the women and children. Years after he departed and the book about the disaster, *A Night to Remember*, was published, Lee Bing appeared in the survivors' list.

You couldn't properly hear the Salvation Army Band until you passed Tait and Kitchen Hardware at Main and Ainslie. The store still had horse collars hanging from hooks in the ceiling. Across the intersection in front of the magnificent sandstone Victorian Gore Insurance building, now appallingly demolished, my future brother-in-law, Roy Petty, hawked late-edition *Toronto Stars*, shouting his wares between numbers by the Salvation Army. The band, mellow and forgiving, attracted crowds of the faithful, including Vart Vartanian in the town's first zoot suit.

"How's the suit fit, Vart?"

"The pants are a bit snug under the armpits."

Between hymns while the pastor delivered admonishments, the bandsmen set their horns, bells down, on the pavement. One subzero night after a long admonishment a cornet player got his tongue frozen in his mouthpiece and had to make his way into Rouse's Music Store, blurting chromatically through his horn for warm water.

The pastor preached against gambling straight at Griffith's Smoke Shop just 100 feet away on Mill Street across from the bus station. You couldn't see into Griffith's because of Sweet Caporal cigarette ads covering its show windows. Only if you sneaked a look when the front door opened could you see the gaming tables through the blue haze.

On Saturday, Hockey Night in Canada, patrons of Griffith's called in bets period by period from a pay phone just inside the front door. One night Reuben Brown, owner of a downtown ladies' shop, was trying to place a bet when the Salvation Army Band struck up "Throw

Out the Lifeline." Reuben, enraged, charged into the street and shouted, "Shut up! I can't hear a damn thing!" And ran back to the phone. He had a voice like a foghorn.

Up the street from Rouse's you might pause at Struthers and Church Feeds to watch children ride the little hopper cars on rails delivering bags of feed to the curb. Next was Joan's Lunch reeking of french fries, and Percy Cline's Men's Wear Shop. For working men. Percy preached against extravagance and high fashion from behind the cash register, his riveting gaze aimed either over his spectacles riding the tip of his nose or under them riding on his forehead. I can't recall ever seeing him look through them. His advertisements in the *Galt Reporter* became collector's items. One ad said: "Percy Cline's Pants Are Down. Come and See His Underwear."

The no man's land between the Iroquois and Royal hotels offered the most exciting albeit hazardous entertainment. Here fights in both hotels spilled into the street and intermingled so that combatants wound up fighting strangers. A policeman watching the fights from a safe distance would be called back to headquarters in the old City Hall on Dickson Street by one dong of the clock tower bell. "Constable Steele," the desk sergeant would say, "we have a report of a fight at the corner of Wellington and Main … again."

"Yes, sir!" And Steele would slow-walk back to where he had come from in time to see the fight broken up by girlfriends of the combatants.

Both hotels ventilated their beverage rooms with large Bessemer fans that blasted beer fumes, cigarette smoke, bowel gas, and cockroaches at head level into the street with a roar that made children cry. My father told me with apparent belief that these fans had power enough to lower the barometric pressure in the beverage rooms and contributed to violence by giving the alcohol a high-altitude effect.

While the fights raged a man wearing buckskins and a ten-gallon hat hawked snake oil beside the Royal Hotel at the corner of Wellington. His white goatee made him all the more distinguished. He called himself the Colonel and resembled the colonel who today sells Kentucky Fried Chicken. His snake liniment, registered in Ottawa under the Patent Medicine Act, was formulated by Ben Sossin at his pharmacy a block away on the corner of Wellington and Dickson.

George Schaller, Ben's assistant, did the mixing and bottling. The base ingredient, George said, was turpentine. To this he added a measure of oil of mustard for that burning sensation essential to healing, camphor for cooling and, most important, a dash of oil tar that created little black specks that sank to the bottom of the bottle and became the mark of authenticity.

The Colonel cautioned people never to buy snake oil if it didn't have those little black specks. The real stuff would cure arthritis, gout, gallstones, and most ladies' ailments too sensitive to mention. It wasn't supposed to be ingested internally, he said, as it might terminate all of your problems.

Ladies making purchases from the Colonel didn't notice the four-foot live blue racer snake he had draped around his neck until it looked them in the eye. Their screams attracted more customers. The Colonel lived rent-free with several pet snakes right across the street from his outlet in a cozy little one-room packing crate nestled between Wilson's Discount Oil Depot, the Canadian National Railways tracks, and a Chinese laundry that later became Kirkham's Appliance Store.

When the Colonel died of undisclosed causes, he left his secret formula to Ben Sossin, who arranged the funeral and bought the headstone. Orders for Blue Racer Liniment increased, however, and George Schaller mixed it by the gallon. Ben cut the price from $1 a bottle to 50 cents and sold it by the case.

3

Adam Ainslie and His Street

The names of the four principal streets enclosing downtown Galt's business section were dictated by ego and political hierarchy. Main Street, of course, was hands-off to avoid expensive and tedious litigation between the village's founding fathers as to who was number one. Water Street, aptly named because it ran beside the

Grand River, caused no dispute because no one wanted his name on a street that flooded every year. William Dickson, who arrived in 1816 with Absalom Shade, laid claim to Dickson Street because it flooded only halfway and ran up past the municipal offices. Shade, a carpenter by trade, built every important building and so had the village, Shade's Mills, named after him. However, John Galt, better connected politically, had the village renamed after him in 1825, and poor Shade had to settle for Shade Street, which ran from the top of Main Street to a cow pasture later to become Soper Park.

The whole region, including Galt, Preston, and Hespeler, was later inexplicably renamed after a British Austin automobile called the Cambridge.

Ainslie Street, flooded only now and then, cut from north to south through the heart of the village and was named after a transient lawyer who happened to be delivering mail. Adam Ainslie was returning to Hamilton from Waterloo where he had gone to deliver some mail to friends who had accompanied him on a ship from Gibraltar. He had walked to Waterloo from Hamilton through Beverly Swamp where travellers had been known to disappear.

At the junction of two muddy paths called Hunter's Corner, now the savage and virtually impassable intersection of Water Street, Dundas Street, Hespeler Road, and Coronation Boulevard, Ainslie refuelled at Hunter's Tavern. He asked Hunter where he might buy a pair of dry socks and was directed down a narrow mucky path from where at a point now covered with Galt Collegiate Institute students' cigarette butts, he caught his first glimpse of the Grand River shimmering in the moonlight.

Ainslie slogged down the path until he reached the intersection of Main and Water streets. At the northeast end of the bridge he entered Absalom Shade's White Store (cash only) and bought from a clerk named Harris, after whom Harris Street would be named, the dry socks. Harris advised Ainslie that he might change his socks in the lounge of the Galt Hotel, run by a fellow named Barlow, predecessor of a cartage company and a future member of the provincial legislature. At the hotel Ainslie changed his socks before a roaring fire and chatted with a pleasant man named Thomas Rich, after whom Rich Avenue would someday be named.

Adam Ainslie was so taken by the hospitality of the village that he decided to stay and have a street named after himself. It helped that he became head of the local militia.

4

Fun and Fear Before Television

In the 1930s and 1940s small-town streets were illuminated mainly by 250-watt bulbs every 100 feet or so on hydro poles. The bare bulbs were screwed under corrugated metal reflectors that were painted white on the underside and resembled straw hats. The flickering twenty-five-cycle current allowed wan circles of light under the bulbs and dark shadowy spaces in between where a person might stand unseen.

Children loved to play games in these checkered spaces of light and dark: hide-and-seek, kick the can, et cetera. And because the streets were as safe as the unlocked churches, parents trying to listen to their radios over the noise of children wrestling in the living room would say, "It's dark now. Why don't you kids run outside and play until it's time for bed?"

The long nights of autumn when the sun set before seven allowed the boys on Lowrey Avenue and Chalmers Street to prowl the town before bedtime. Sometimes we stuck close to home and goaded selected fleet-footed men into chasing us. We did this simply by tapping on their front doors.

Art Snutch was always good for a wild chase. He terrified us and we loved it. Art lived in a tiny red brick house across from Dykeman's Variety Store on the corner of Lowrey and Pollock. One tap on his door and he was on top of us, legs scissoring in the air, hollering, "I'll tan your hides!" He was tall, thin, and bandy-legged and could run like a deer. Ivan McQueen, who lived half a block away beside Lincoln Avenue Church, occasionally joined Snutch in the chase. Ivan, a bit paunchy and not as fleet as Art, had an ominous bass voice that threatened us from the sky. One night Art and Ivan crashed together in the dark, fell down, and limped home, holding their heads. We knew better than to laugh.

Weekend nights and a later curfew led us across town to Victoria Park and on to the spring beside the Canadian Pacific Railway tracks in Barrie's Cut. There was a campsite there, where during the Depression men in search of work dropped from freight trains to rest for a night and share a can of beans. We reached the campsite by following a scrub-lined path that led from the top of Victoria Park to the tracks. As soon as we saw the firelight through the brambles, we dropped to our hands and knees and, like Indians, stalked the campsite until we heard the voices and smelled cigarette smoke. There was laughter and singing and sometimes a harmonica. All the men at the campsite were off westbound freights upgrade. The eastbound freights were too fast to get on or off.

Invariably, while we lurked in the grass, a westbound freight would come blasting up the grade, double-headed by steam engines with different-size drive wheels and nervous out-of-synch exhausts. After the long, doleful whistle at Blenheim Road, the cannonading exhausts blotted out all other sounds. One of us, startled by a rabbit bounding by and sensing heavier steps, would leap up and run, touching off a general panic that sent everyone racing back down the trail, shrieking and leaping over the fallen until, back in the park, we slumped gasping to the ground close to the deer enclosure where everything seemed safe.

Grenfell Davenport would say, "That was a close one. Anyone missing?"

5

Beware Gentle Percy

The deer enclosure was Percy Hill's pet. He was superintendent of the Galt Parks Board in the 1940s. The enclosure extended hundreds of feet into the hardwoods from the duck pond and allowed visitors to watch deer run in close to natural surroundings. The duck pond hosted a variety of tamed birds that shrieked, squawked, and honked everyone out of their beds within earshot at dawn each day. There were also platoons of multi-coloured rabbits that took leave to visit gardens for blocks around. Percy loved animals and nature.

Most Saturday mornings he sat in the Morris chair in my parents' kitchen and discussed begonias and peat moss with my dad who had a little greenhouse leaning on the garage. Pop sold him geranium slippings.

Percy was tall, slim, soft-spoken, and gentle and gave much thought to the ways of the universe, but God help anyone who crossed him up. One morning he sat in the Morris chair with our cat purring in his lap and recounted with relish the fate of people who stole firewood.

He and the men who tended Victoria Park trimmed dead wood and burnt it in their own fireplaces. They stacked the wood at the end of the service lane behind the deer pens and took it home at their leisure. Every time they got a nice pile together, however, someone stole it. Percy, figuring the thieves came in the dead of night, rigged a trap for them. He drove four-inch spikes through a plank and laid it across the lane in front of the woodpile, spikes down during the day, but up at night. For weeks nothing happened. Then one morning Percy went in to find the wood stolen again. The spikes were up, but the wood was gone.

Later that morning he went for gas at Mil's Service Station at the foot of Blenheim Road. The attendant at the pumps told Percy he had seen something that morning that he hadn't seen in thirty years at the service station. A little pickup truck limped in with four flat tires. Yes, it was carrying a load of wood. Percy took the spiked plank away. The wood was never stolen again.

6

Crocodiles in Soper Park

Soper Park was the favourite summer haunt of developing boys because we could swim under the murky water of Mill Creek and grope the girls. It was also the site of the world's largest peony plot, confirmed by Earl Werstine in his *Galt Reporter* column several times each spring. Horticulturists came in buses to visit the peony plot. I always intended to visit it myself but never did. Just below the world's largest peony plot a merry-go-round serenaded the big kids frolicking in the upper-creek bathing pool. The big kids ranged in age from thirteen to thirty-seven if you counted Tink Clark.

We used to hide behind the spirea bushes and watch the big boys play. Everything they did led up to throwing the big girls into the creek. The girls were always in the way, preening themselves on blankets right where the boys wanted to wrestle. Constable Steele, patrolling on his bicycle, would watch the big kids from behind the spirea, too. He smiled.

Inspired by the big kids, we would run down to the lower pool by the Dundas Street tunnel where the little kids swam. The little kids ranged in age from five to thirty-six if you counted Tink Clark's brother, Da Da. The lower pool was a great place to play crocodile. The object of the game was to slide through the water with just our eyes showing, like crocodiles, and grab the girls ... some of whom were visibly developing ... and pull them under. The girls pretended to hate this and called out to their mothers.

I recounted these good times recently with Janet Elliott of St. George. "I always knew you were a crocodile," she said. "Wes Lillie was another. And that Grenfell Davenport. My mother wanted to kill you." In those days boys were always in danger of being killed by someone's mother, sometimes their own. Janet said she got water up her nose and that her sinuses hadn't been right since. "You pinched, too," she said, getting shrill, "and you haven't changed."

7
Tink Clark Dazzles Leafs

When I was a boy, the chance of seeing a National Hockey League team at training camp was remote. So when Wes Lillie said, "Let's go down to the arena and watch the Toronto Maple Leafs work out," I thought he was kidding. But he said it had to be true because his father, Frank, had heard it from Abby Kilgour, the Galt arena rink supervisor.

So down we went on a Saturday morning: Wes, his sister, Lois, and half a dozen boys from Lowrey Avenue. No trouble getting in. No security, no passes. Wes just spoke to Abby, and he said sure, but not to be pests and no autographs. We seemed to be the only spectators, and for our exclusive viewing, spread out before us like the players on one of those tabletop hockey games, were the Leafs, including Syl Apps, Dit Clapper, Gordie Drillon, Red Horner, and Turk Broda — names that Foster Hewitt hollered at us all winter.

We crouched like field mice behind the glass at the southeast corner of the rink, just below the gondola where, twenty-two years down the road, Wes Lillie, like Foster Hewitt, would call the play-by-play radio account of the Galt Hornets chasing the Allan Cup. During a skirmish, one of the Leafs' players broke a stick and kicked it to the boards. Immediately, a youth leaped from a gate, skated madly down the rink, picked up the stick, and streaked back, stopping in a great spray of ice chips like Rocket Richard.

"That," said Wes, "is Tink Clark."

His real name was Ernie, but everyone called him Tink. He didn't belong to the Leafs. He was one of Abby Kilgour's "rink rats." As such, he helped Abby water the ice (the Zamboni machine had yet to be invented), clean up the aisles and washrooms, and lead with a baton the Grand March on roller-skating nights.

A lot of kids made fun of Tink because he wasn't what you would call a Rhodes Scholar. He just wasn't cut out for school. Tink was born to tend that rink and did so superbly for more than thirty years, long after the Leafs there that day had retired.

The following Saturday we crept in to see the whole Maple Leafs team sitting on the boards watching what appeared to be a power-skating demonstration. It was Tink Clark clearing the ice with his wooden scraper. He was really flying and grinning from ear to ear. It had to be his finest moment, clearing that ice surface faster than any man alive while all the Leafs watched and marvelled. When he finished, one of the Leafs' players took the scraper and had a try pushing it. He shook his head. The Leafs didn't know it, but they had just had a preview of Eddie Shack.

8

Yes, Suh, No, Suh

During the Depression of the 1930s, a lot of guys hung out at Tate's Smoke Shop near the delta on Water Street. There wasn't much else to do. Tate liked company and set two benches outside and two inside for the men to sit. The outside men handled the gas pump, took in the cash, and carried out the change. Tate considered it beneath his dignity to do this. He was a respected businessman. A bookie, in fact.

Bing McCauley recalls riding his tricycle to Tate's to play his harmonica for treats. "Little Brown Jug" was good for an ice-cream cone, and "Melancholy Baby" might bring a chocolate bar. Sometimes one of the men would join him on the spoons. Another might sing or do a little jig.

Bing says Tate always wore a fedora on the back of his head, though he never stepped outside. And he called everybody "suh."

"Yes, suh. Thank you, suh." That was about the limit of his conversation except when he talked about the horses. When a woman not familiar with the shop was addressed as "suh," she would look around

27

to see if he was talking to a man behind her. Then she would hurry out the door. "Thank you, suh," Tate would holler after her.

Bing, who developed into an accomplished jazz piano player, credits Tate's Smoke Shop with launching his musical career.

9

What Winters We Had — Heroics on the Hills

Today's young drivers are thrilled and bored by accounts of heroic battles with snow during the greatly exaggerated and legendary winters of sixty years ago, but here goes, anyway. Weather forecasts then were much more hopeless than they are today, and blizzards struck without warning at peak traffic hours. It seemed that the storms always began at 4:00 p.m. so that every able-bodied boy and flirtatious girl in Central School could run to the foot of the hill there to watch the cars slide out of control. Roads weren't salted then, and trucks with sand never arrived until after the emergency crews at the Board of Works had finished supper. So the five o'clock rush guaranteed bedlam on every hill in Galt. Central School Hill was the worst because of its sharp ascending curves.

Most cars in those days sported sets of chains on their rear-drive wheels to dig traction out of the ice. All police cars and fire trucks did. But there were always enough cars without chains to cause gridlock. Wheel chains were outlawed with the advent of snow tires and the realization that the chains were shredding the asphalt.

Anyway, the jams on the hills enabled schoolboys to demonstrate their new-found strength and chivalry. They would take hold of a car spinning its wheels and sliding sideways and, with pubescent roars, shoulder it up the hill. Whenever a boy lost his footing and fell face down in the slush, another would leap in to grab the fender. Girls would squeal. Boys in grades seven and eight, like the Mills brothers,

Donald and Ray, and Billy Schultz performed feats of strength that risked landing them in the army. Tink Clark, just thirty-seven in grade eight, appeared to lift the rear ends of cars right off the ground.

Not many women drove cars then, but whenever one of them tackled the hill the boys would abandon the men they were pushing and rush to the lady's aid, knocking one another down in their hurry to get there, Vart Vartanian leading the pack. After five the guys drifting home from the beer parlours joined and you would swear that some of them were actually pushing cars *down* the hill.

Reports from other hills, Concession Street and St. Andrews were favourites, arrived by runner. The mess there it seemed was always worse than on our hill. Fire trucks were colliding with police cars and ambulances.

One snowy afternoon there actually was a fire at the top of Central School Hill, and the firemen couldn't get up through the jam. The fire was just over the fence from the schoolyard, on Bruce Street, in a little shed where a man with bulging eyes, a sort of hermit, fixed radios. The firemen didn't have wireless communication in their trucks so there was a lot of shouting back and forth as to who was to do what and go where. Boys ran up and down the hill hollering contradictory rumours. There was an explosion. People were jumping out of windows.

At last Grenfell Davenport, running like a deer, ended the confusion. The fire was out, he hollered. He and a pack of boys had put it out with snowballs.

10

A Child's Christmas on Havill Street

When Grandma and Grandpa Spring were still with us, we had Christmas dinner at their house on Havill Street in

Galt. Before dinner we exchanged gifts in the parlour. Only one person at a time was allowed to open a gift and everyone would say "Ooh!" and "Ah!" as if they were at a fireworks display. After dinner the adults retired to the kitchen, leaving the children to play with their new toys or eavesdrop through the closed kitchen door. My mother and all my aunts had the gift of hysterical laughter, and when we heard that through the door we knew our uncles were telling jokes.

That done there was a hush while Aunt Sisley Alsop told stories of mystery and imagination. She was a spiritualist preacher in California and came every Christmas with a bag of messages from the dead. Gasps came through the door. Next came squeals when she read palms. It wasn't what you would call an orthodox Christmas.

While my aunts did the dinner dishes and recounted difficult births, and before the poker game started, the uncles and larger nephews charged out to the street in a cloud of cigar smoke for a snowball fight. Strange now to recall Uncle John, the decrepit old man I sat watching hockey games with years later, running down Havill Street to snowball the fedora off Uncle Ted.

Every other Christmas, instead of playing poker after dinner and the snowball fight, the adults would indulge in a few games of bingo. This was in lieu of prayer and carol singing, which gives you some idea of where we stood on the social scale.

Uncle Fred Linder, in spite of stammering worse than anyone I have ever heard, insisted on calling the bingo. It was a challenge that everyone conceded. Anyway, he owned all the bingo paraphernalia (cards, a revolving cage that released the numbered Ping-Pong balls, et cetera). One year he forgot to bring the bingo equipment, and my father drove him home to pick it up in our 1929 Chevrolet.

On the return trip Uncle Fred, possibly because of my father's flatulence, chose to ride outside on the running board. My father cornered onto Havill Street too fast for Uncle Fred to hang on, and he flew off and torpedoed through the slush headfirst into the snow banked along the curb. They slogged into the house, howling with laughter. Uncle Fred's fedora was caked with slush and squished down around his ears. We all howled at the sight of him.

When Uncle Fred recounted what had happened, our mouths dropped and we fell silent. Not because of his near-death experience, but because he had stopped stammering. For half an hour he talked just like us. My mother, who believed that Uncle Fred stammered because he ran a machine gun during World War I, told my sister, Shirley, and me that this was our father's first miracle.

Sadly, it didn't last. The stammering, worse if anything, returned as soon as Uncle Fred began to call the bingo. My mother said this was the Lord's way of telling us we were desecrating his birthday.

After Grandma and Grandpa Spring died, Christmas moved to Auntie Bea's house just around the corner on Concession Street. Auntie Bea married late in life and met her husband at a bingo. She never won at bingo, my mother said, but the man she met became another Uncle Bill.

Theirs was a stillborn marriage. Auntie Bea remained a spinster and Uncle Bill, sexually frustrated, continually tested their love by threatening to die. It was his good fortune to develop a minor heart condition that required popping a nitroglycerine pill before and after every exertion when Auntie Bea was around. "I'm taking out the garbage, darling," he would holler as he popped a nitro into his mouth with a flourish. "If I'm not back in five minutes, you'll know that I've dropped." Sometimes in a pique she would dare him to go ahead and drop and he would say, "You'd like that, wouldn't you, sweetheart? Well, I might just be around for years."

They tormented each other through Thanksgiving dinner, and we all braced ourselves for the crash, possibly headfirst into the potato salad. But at Christmas they always managed a truce, like the one on the Western Front in France in 1914.

Ours wasn't a drinking family except for two uncles, one great-uncle, and three cousins, so Christmas never got out of control. Auntie Bea, however, after one sip of wine, would do a little dance by herself until she got dizzy and fell onto the sofa.

A Salvation Army major lived next door, and Auntie Bea took great pains to hide from him the fact that any alcohol entered her house. One year, a couple of days before Christmas, she was nursing a large bottle of wine from the bus stop when she came upon the major shovelling the snow off her front walk. She hid the bottle under her coat and stopped to thank him. They talked of charity and sobriety for several minutes before she lost her grip and the bottle smashed at his feet. She told my mother she couldn't think of a single thing to say while the major helped her pick up the broken glass. My mother said she should have told him her husband had made her buy it, but Auntie Bea lacked the guile.

11
Good Cheer at the Station

Over Christmas and New Year's the Galt Canadian Pacific Railway station is now the bleakest place in town. Even the freight trains take a holiday. The depot sits dark and silent. What a contrast to the days of passenger trains and steam engines in the 1940s and 1950s when the station was the liveliest place in town.

Hundreds of people went there just to watch passengers coming and going, especially on weekends. Orville Rumble, who wore sunglasses day and night, summer and winter, went there to scout new ladies coming to town. Fish in wooden crates arrived, too, from Port Dover, and Lake Erie and Northern electric cars made it up to the station on a spur line. On holiday weekends sightseers parked their cars on Rose Street and walked to the station. Taxis crowded the parking space close to the platform. Galt Cab, Fraser's Taxi, De Luxe Cab, and Preston Taxi flocked to the station at train time like gulls to a fish boat.

Holiday trains came in two sections fifteen minutes apart. The first section, made up of old wooden coaches, carried college students. There was a lot of singing on board, and on occasion someone would blow a bugle out the door. The second section, comprised of steel coaches, carried the establishment: businessmen wearing mohair coats, ladies sporting fur hats, magnates in club cars full of cigar smoke, and sometimes in the last two coaches, the Toronto Maple Leafs or Detroit Red Wings hockey teams.

On a Saturday night in winter, back when the late-edition *Toronto Star* arrived by train, paperboys and girls ran circles around cars as they heaved snowballs. The station had a general waiting room and a separate ladies' waiting room, presumably a sanctuary for spinsters and nuns and other custodians of virginity. The beer parlours downtown were similarly divided.

"Here she comes!" someone would shout at the first sign of the headlight rising in the east, and everyone in the waiting rooms would rise as if for a hymn, lift their luggage, and jam through the doors to the platform. The awesome steam engines rolled in, bells clanging, brakes screeching, drive rods scissoring over six-foot drive wheels, their weight rattling the station windows.

Westbound trains were usually double-headed, and the smoke from the two engines often made the station disappear in a swirl of sulphurous gas and steam sweetly garnished with superheated valve oil. Little boys and their fathers gathered by the locomotives to bask in the heat and watch the engineer, a celebrity at every stop, oil the drive-rod knuckles and tap the pumps and shafts with a heavy steel mallet here and there like a doctor sounding a patient's chest.

The conductor hollered "All aboard" and tugged on a cord to sound a peanut whistle in the locomotive cab to tell the engineer to activate the bell and release the brakes. What a thrill to hear those great engines bark and blast their volcanic exhausts skyward, a sight that today would drive environmentalists crazy. Coach after coach slid by faster and faster as did the heads of passengers peering out until suddenly all was quiet and a ghost of steam and red markers faded off across the Grand River bridge.

I remember, as a boy, lying in bed at night listening to freights rumble across the bridge and charge with staccato exhausts up the steep grade to Orr's Lake. The whistle at Blenheim Road crossing let you know when the engines were about to pass the spring where the hobos camped as the trains battled the toughest stretch of the grade through Barrie's Cut. The exhausts would slow and sometimes one of the engines would lose its grip and spin its wheels and exhaust like a machine gun until the engineer throttled back and fed more sand to the rails. Sometimes the grade won. The exhausts slowed until the next seemed as if it had to be the last. But there was always one more, and then another. When at last the train gave up, there would be two toots on the whistle and the growing rumble as the engines backed their load down the hill and into the Galt yards for another run.

Frendy Graham, who handled baggage and express for years at the Galt station, said he remembered at least two occasions when engines took off up the grade without their trains, the engineers not realizing it until they reached Orr's Lake siding. With two engines it was sometimes hard to know which one was doing all the pulling.

It is difficult to realize that two generations of people have never seen a steam train. Those of us lucky enough to have witnessed them and ridden on them can never forget. With a little imagination, as I nod off at night, I can still hear them.

12

Express Lobsters

Frendy Graham's favourite train passengers were the Nova Scotia lobsters that passed through Galt en route to the Palmer House Hotel in Chicago. He didn't have to check them through, but he ate quite a lot of them. An express handler on the train carrying the lobsters, Frank "Slippery" Morrison, always plucked a couple of live ones from their crushed ice crate and passed them to Frendy in a paper bag. Rod MacLeod, the station operator, plopped them into a pot of boiling water, and the two dined on them after the train pulled out.

"Boy, were they ever good!" Frendy said. "Whenever I met people going to Chicago, I would tell them to be sure to get the lobster at the Palmer House. Slippery, or Slip as we called him, was a wiry little Irishman who loved people. He had a degree from the University of

Dublin but preferred working on the trains. Sometimes he got off and did an Irish jig on the platform. He also sold light bulbs on the side."

One night after Slip handed Frendy his bag of lobsters, CPR London division superintendent Art Tees stepped down from the train for a chat. While the chat went on the lobsters were trying to claw their way out of the bag. To avoid the embarrassment of having a lobster grab Tees by the thumb, Frendy excused himself to move a couple of suitcases and tossed the bag into the flowerbed surrounding the illuminated Galt sign.

After Tees departed on the train, all Frendy could find in the flowerbed was an empty bag. He searched frantically in the dark until he caught the lobsters crawling down the lawn in the general direction of the New Albion Hotel.

Frendy suspected that he and MacLeod weren't the only station crew Slip treated to lobster. He probably gave some to the guys at Guelph Junction, too. And Woodstock and London and Chatham and Windsor. Maybe he even took a couple to Rosie's Bar, his favourite haunt in Detroit. And there was always a pot boiling in the baggage car. Who knows, maybe he even shared a few with Art Tees? Whatever, the kitchen staff at the Palmer House must have wondered why they kept getting crates of nothing but crushed ice from Nova Scotia.

13

Taxi

If, when you hopped from a passenger train in those steamy days of yesterday, you hailed a Deluxe Cab, your driver might have been Willis Toles who, if he had jazz on the radio, would sit in the driver's seat, stomping his foot, and leave you to open the door yourself. "Heave your suitcase in the trunk," he would holler, "and slam the lid because the lock sticks."

If you hailed a Galt cab, your driver might have been George Goshgarian, a slim, soft-spoken philosopher who, if it was a nice day and you weren't burdened with suitcases, would try to talk you into walking home. He would turn in the driver's seat, fix you with dark Armenian eyes, and say, "People should walk more," as if he had just carried the message down from Mount Ararat. "Are you sure you want this ride?"

If you insisted, he would start the engine, but it was a philosophy lesson all the way home. "I don't mind driving farmers home," he would say, "because I know they are going to be pitching hay. But city people are getting too fat. Look at that big slob standing on the corner. How many years do you think he has left?"

As a young adult commuting to Toronto, I always looked for George when I got off the train. One beautiful Saturday morning I lugged a large suitcase over to his cab. He hopped out, opened the rear door, and put the suitcase on the seat. "Ride to 16 Lowrey, eh!" he said, giving the blue sky an appreciative glance. "That's about two miles. When I was in the army, we'd consider it a treat to march only two miles on a sunny day." He had been a corporal in the Royal Engineers in World War II. His brother, James, died as an air gunner with the Royal Canadian Air Force. "Why don't I drop your suitcase off on your front porch while you walk it? I won't charge the fare."

I told him I wanted to get home right away to walk a dog who was waiting for me. He smiled so that I knew he didn't believe me and opened the other door.

George always smoked when he was driving, but blew it out the draftless vent so that it didn't bother you. "I'd offer you a cigarette," he'd say, "but people smoke too much for their own good."

One morning I got off the 10:20 from Toronto and shared George's cab with three dapper businessmen carrying briefcases and assorted luggage. It was customary to share cabs even when you were jammed in. Nowhere was far to go, and the fare was a straight 50 cents a head. The businessmen wanted to check into the Iroquois Hotel. I merely wanted a ride downtown. They asked George to wait outside the hotel while they checked in their luggage and then drive them to the Gore Insurance office on Dundas Street.

"Shame you've got that luggage," George said. "It's such a nice day to walk." And then he turned those hypnotic dark eyes on them. "But you could walk from the hotel to the Gore. If you did that, you could stop in at my sister's restaurant on Shade Street for a bite to eat. It's called Palvetzian's. She might even whip you up an Armenian dish. And after that you could walk past our arena gardens, home of the Allan Cup champion Galt Terriers, and see Soper Park, which is full of children playing baseball. Lovely walk."

We piled out at the Iroquois. George winked at me to indicate that I didn't have to pay, then helped the men carry in their bags. I waited to see what would happen when they came out. I couldn't hear what was said as they conferred beside the cab, but apparently George won out. He pointed across the Canadian National Railways tracks towards Shade Street and waved the three goodbye as they set off, smiling, on foot.

I always imagined that George, with his stress-free approach to life, would be with us promoting fitness into his nineties. But he was buried on his seventieth birthday. According to his niece, Nevi Palvetzian, his chain-smoking did him in. That and a lack of exercise. Stuck in his cab all day he didn't walk enough.

14

The Radio Inspectors

*J*ust for the archives: is there a person alive who has actually seen a radio inspector? This isn't a question for anyone born after World War II. Before the war, radios were considered luxuries to be taxed. I believe it was $2 a year, and it was hated as much as today's GST.

Everyone but the Mennonites had a radio, so you had to cough up for at least one licence. It was the fees for the second and third radios that people tried to avoid.

Our one declared radio stood like a little veneer cathedral in the living room. The unlicensed ones were in my parents' bedroom, the bathroom, and Pop's dilapidated greenhouse. I remember Pop telling Mom with alarm in his voice, "Alec Rouse just called to say the radio licence inspector has been spotted on Lincoln Avenue." One block away!

Alec Rouse had a radio repair business in Rouse's Music Store, which he shared with his brother, Gordon, who repaired washing machines and later became mayor of Galt. On Saturday night when the Salvation Army Band played right outside their front door, customers in the store had to shout.

Alec lived just three doors north of us on Lowrey Avenue and took upon himself the responsibility of warning the whole block of the radio inspector's approach. My dad reacted to the alert the way people in Germany were reacting to the Gestapo. "Hide the bedroom radio in the hall closet!" he would holler to Mom. "And stick the bathroom radio under the straw in the fruit cellar!" Then he would run out and hide the greenhouse radio under some fish flats in a coldframe.

The alert touched off quite a flurry of housecleaning on the block. Everybody seemed to have a carton of trash for the garage. The telephone operators, who listened in all the time and knew everything, passed the alert to the whole town. In some houses disconnected aerial and ground wires dangled in every room. After a couple of days, Alec Rouse, mysteriously informed, would sound the all-clear and the radios would come out of hiding.

Oddly enough, no one ever saw a radio licence inspector. A boy might say that his aunt had talked to one on Pollock Avenue and that he was knocking on doors, but by the time we ran over there the street was empty. I asked my dad how a person could recognize a radio inspector, and he said they looked like bailiffs and walked through the Legion Hall without taking their hats off.

15

Treasured Discipline

Passing Central School in Galt and seeing the children playing with their lawyers at recess takes me down Memory Lane to when we had playground justice without litigation or emergency

38

meetings of the Home and School Association. It was quick, decisive, illegal, and effective.

Central School discipline, like discipline in all the schools in those golden days, would serve now as an on-site demonstration of every possible parent-teacher-pupil and accessory legal action for articling lawyers' enrichment days. Safety, another of today's legal minefields, was an aberration practised by girls. Boys, especially in the presence of girls, flouted safety.

We didn't have condom machines in the schools sixty years ago, so there was little to do at recess but defy death. In winter the steep hill that Central School sits on became one huge slide. We slid, bumping our heads on iron posts, down the concrete walk leading from the upper to the lower yard. And we slid down the ash heap that Mr. Campbell, the school janitor, dumped out of the furnace room tunnel.

The most life-threatening slide was the concrete drain trough running from the upper walkway straight down to the lower playground. We called it "the chute," and it would drop you sixty feet in five seconds. The only way down the chute without ripping your pants to shreds and endangering your ability to procreate was to squat on one heel and stick your free leg out in front of you in a manner most likely to break it. Only the bravest boys and wildest girls risked the plunge. The only girl I remember doing it regularly was Janet Winter, later Ms. Elliott of St. George, where she did even more dangerous things.

Teachers on yard duty blew whistles to stop the sliding on the chute long enough to clear away piles of children at the bottom. The chief enforcer for a couple of years was a grade four teacher named Mr. Pleasant (I am not making this up), a virtuoso with the strap. If he caught you loading a snowball with a rock, he would strap you thrice on each hand — hard. He strapped boys in lines of four and five with a foot-long length of rubber brake lining laced with asbestos fibres. A lawsuit today involving a schoolboy strapped with asbestos fibres would fill page one of the *Toronto Sun* for a week. One day word went around that Grenfell Davenport had pulled his hand back so that Mr. Pleasant hit his own knee. That was one of the times Grenfell hid for a couple of days in McBain's barn.

One thing you didn't do for sure, though it is commonly done today even by lawyers, was throw a snowball at a girl. When Boyd Shewan, the principal, caught a boy tossing a snowball at a girl, he stuck two fingers in his mouth and sounded a whistle that stiffened even Mr. Pleasant. All playground activity ceased, and the guilty boy was led to face the wooden schoolyard fence. Mr. Shewan, hand raised and eye on his watch, would shout "Fire!" and 200 crazed boys would paste the condemned to the fence with a withering barrage of snowballs — the firing squad. He stopped the barrage after precisely two minutes with another piercing whistle. On a good packing day the wet snowballs hit the fence like horses' hoofs. Imagine in this day of law and order trying to get a jury to a schoolyard on a good packing day.

That we survived such primitive and lawless times explains why seniors today are so tough and never complain about anything. And where were the lawyers when we needed them? Probably throwing snowballs at the boy pinned to the fence. One thing about those golden days, though, was that we kids never had to pass through metal detectors.

16

Slingshot Justice

In 1928, when Al Capone was shooting up Chicago with machine guns, a gang of twelve-year-old boys roamed our neighbouring town of Hespeler, shooting out streetlights with slingshots. The slingshot (ask Goliath) is a lethal weapon, and today boys would be forced to register them.

One sunny day Odele Gehiere, his brother, Arsiene, Cecil Proud, Billy Black, Ernie Lee, and Archie Scott armed at the gravel pit behind Hillcrest School and swaggered down Queen Street with pockets full of stones as round and smooth as robins' eggs. They were sly enough not to shoot at anything in broad daylight, but Arsiene Gehiere, testing the feel of a stone in his sling, lost his grip and accidentally fired the round through the front window of a house owned by a man notorious for his hatred of little boys.

The man charged into the street in a frothing rage, ordered the boys to stand where they were, and ran back into his house to call the police. The police at that time consisted of Chief Tom Wilson. The chief had a jail but no patrol car and had to call George Woods's taxi service to deliver him to the sites of crime. Failing to get a coherent explanation for the broken window at the site, the chief made the boys march ahead of the taxi the few blocks to the police station in the town hall.

There he drew a confession from Arsiene Gehiere and demanded to know how such an "accident" could happen. Gehiere loaded his slingshot with a choice stone and stretched the rubber. "It just slipped from my fingers," he said, "like this." And the stone shot across the room straight through the frosted glass on the door that said Chief of Police. The chief, adjusting his face, marched the six boys into a jail cell and held them there for one hour.

Archie Scott said the boys' parents had to pay for both windows but couldn't remember how much they cost. The brief jail term seemed to straighten out the boys. Archie told me this story just a few years back, and he was still law-abiding. Indeed none of the boys involved embarked on a life of crime except Ernie Lee who, I am told, joined the Tory Party.

George Woods, the taxi driver, told me he drove Chief Wilson to crime sites, usually the local beer parlours, and to the jail for years, even helping him carry drunks to the cells, and never once billed the town for his services. That was the way things were done then. After George served as deputy for nearly two years, the chief said to him, "George, some day when you can spare the time it wouldn't be a bad idea to drive down to Galt and get your driver's licence."

17

Bedlam at the Funeral Home

Coutts and Son Funeral Directors in Galt used to be owned and operated by Harold Gray, and during the 1930s and 1940s it was the prestigious way out. Mr. Gray made every effort to sustain the tone of his service — dignified, elegant, and serene, goals he met until he brought his son, Bud, into the business.

Bud, like his father, was rotund and tall, an imposing figure. Bursting with youth, he had the self-discipline of a circus bear cub. He had a friend just as large and even more uncontrollable, who he talked his father into hiring as an assistant. The friend's name was Willis Toles, an accomplished jazz trombone player who could double ably on bass, piano, and guitar; was a veteran cab driver; and was a crack shot with a revolver and consistently beat out the local policemen in marksman competitions.

Business was good, so Mr. Gray had no need for a revolver marksman, but Toles's experience as a cab driver made him a natural to drive the ambulance, a service then in the hands of funeral directors. Bud was assigned to drive the hearse. It wasn't surprising to see the hearse clear St. Andrews Street at sixty miles per hour chased by the ambulance with the siren on. Occasionally, the two would run out for coffee in the ambulance with the siren on. It must have occurred to Mr. Gray that his funeral parlour had been taken over by the Marx Brothers.

When the solemnity of a service was rent by shouting in the yard and hoots of laughter coming from the ambulance garage, Mr. Gray would run out of the chapel, wave his arms wildly, pretend to strangle himself, and run back inside. One day, after Bud banged up a front fender on the hearse, Harold sent Toles down to Bennett City Garage Body Shop to pick it up. He wouldn't trust Bud. Toles brought it back intact, but while nursing it into the garage scraped it from end to end.

Mr. Gray, when he wasn't pretending to strangle himself, was noted for his composure. He finally lost it at a funeral in Sheffield. The service was in an old country church, and Mr. Gray sent Bud and Toles into the basement to keep out of trouble. However, Toles found a piano in the Sunday school room and began to pound out "C Jam Blues." Bud joined in by pounding jam tins with chair rungs. Mourners seated upstairs weren't amused. Neither was Mr. Gray who, really strangling himself, raced downstairs. He couldn't fire his own son, but Toles had to go.

Toles went to work for the opposition, Jimmy Little, when his funeral home was on Grand Avenue. Because Toles lived in a double house on Barrie Street, he wasn't allowed to practise his trombone or bass fiddle at home, so he rehearsed in the embalming room at Little's. On his way to his band job at Leisure Lodge, he would drop into Little's and pick up his bass. One time a passerby, seeing Toles carrying out the casket-size instrument in the dark, thought it was someone stealing bodies and called the police. The officers searched high and low until Jimmy Little assured them the body count was okay.

18

Cinders Tell All

One summer day in 1940, Grenfell Davenport said we should visit Janet Winter who had just moved from a house on east Main Street to a big home on the crescent above Queen's Square. Janet was always moving and going to different schools, but we thought we should keep track of her because she was the only girl we knew who would kiss anybody. She was ten years old.

So we recruited Kenny Lee and Jim Bastin at the East Street dump, where they had been picking over odds and ends, and headed for the crescent on the west side. We found her house by asking where the new girl with the skinny legs lived. She was really pleased to see us and suggested we visit the animal pens in Victoria Park. There she introduced us to two girls who would soon be her classmates at Dickson School.

The sound of a steam train whistle prompted Grenfell to suggest we pop up to Barrie's Cut to visit the spring where the hobos camped. He claimed to have sat by their fire at night and drunk beer with them. So up we went along the trail through the hawthorns (all subdivisions now) and down to the spring. It is still there beside the tracks just south of Simpson's sawmill. There we splashed around until we were pretty well soaked and one of Janet's new friends started to cry.

"Don't worry," Grenfell said. "We can all dry off on the bridge."

Close to the spring a high wooden bridge carried the lane to Linton's farm over the tracks in the cut. It was a favourite thrill of boys to stand on this old bridge and brace the exhaust of a train blasting up the grade. Now we could hear a train rumbling over the Grand River bridge and heading our way. We told the girls we were really in luck, that we could stand on the bridge while the train passed under and dry our clothes really fast.

The girls, except for Janet, didn't like the idea, but Grenfell told them they hadn't lived until they had had steam up their skirts. Janet, who was precocious, said it would at least be safer than sex. So we dared each other onto the bridge and watched the roaring black smoke approach. The wooden bridge planks had two-inch-wide cracks between them, and we positioned the girls over them for their maximum pleasure. Actually, we wanted to see if their light summer skirts would blow up. They couldn't hold them down with their fingers in their ears.

The freight, westbound on the heavy grade, had two locomotives blasting with every pound of steam they could muster. The advancing tornado raised the hair on our necks, and we stuck our fingers in our ears and closed our eyes tight. The lead engine's exhaust shook the bridge and exploded up through the cracks, firing sparks up trousers and skirts. To top it off, the engineer, spotting us, blew his whistle. The power of a steam whistle six feet beneath you is enough to shake the fillings out of your teeth.

We were reeling so much from the first engine that the second, the most powerful, caused the girls to scream. After it passed and the bridge settled down, we stood shaking our heads and patting bituminous gases back down our pant legs. I pried cinders from my eyes.

"My skirt blew up," Janet said. "Did you peek, Grenfell?"

"How could I see with cinders in my eyes?" he asked.

"You wouldn't get cinders in your eyes if you hadn't peeked," she said. "I'm telling my mother."

The only boy who didn't peek was Jim Bastin, who went to the Gospel Hall and could be trusted. Grenfell, Kenny Lee, and I all went to First United and couldn't be trusted. What's more, Kenny, because he wore glasses, didn't get cinders in his eyes and gave us such graphic descriptions of the girls' underwear that we wondered about the state of decency on the west side of town. Jim Bastin even said he wished he had opened his eyes.

We talked about that time on the bridge for weeks afterwards while we picked over odds and ends at the East Street dump. Of course, more sensational things have happened in the years since, but not much more.

19
Professor Thiele

Professor Thiele was the first charismatic person I ever saw. I was with my parents on Water Street trying to see a parade through the legs of a crowd.

Parades in the 1930s were one of the few forms of entertainment people could afford, mainly because they cost nothing. Several bands had gone by, huffing and puffing, and all I saw were flashes of braid and brass. Then someone said, "Here comes Professor Thiele," and the whole crowd rose on tiptoe. His band, the Waterloo Music Society Band, exceptionally precise and powerful, towered above every band that had passed.

I managed to pop my head out from under a fat lady's arm and — pow! There he was, Professor Thiele, the legend, baton in hand, his white uniform gleaming, marching before a wall of trombones. That the band was dressed in dark blue made him gleam in white all the more.

John Mellor, in his biography of Thiele, *Music in the Park*, says the professor and his family, before they immigrated to Canada, were virtually an institution in the United States. Thiele had played with John Philip Sousa and Edwin Goldman and had toured with his own family concert troupe. His wife, Louise, was a cornet virtuoso; was accomplished on the piano, marimbaphone, and clarinet; and was a spellbinder with her dramatic readings. Dramatic readings in those days were the mark of a superior band concert.

So how on earth did they get to Waterloo?

When the United States entered the war against Germany in 1917, anti-German hysteria left Thiele and his family unemployed, even though both he and his wife had been born in America. Broke and desperate, Thiele answered an advertisement in the magazine *Billboard* for a bandmaster in a place called Waterloo, Ontario, Canada, and came up for an interview. As he boarded a train in New York City, he told his wife to buy a French dictionary in case he got the job. "Everybody up there speaks French," he said. A week later, when he returned jubilant with the job, he said, "Throw out that French dictionary, Louise. Believe it or not, up there they all speak German."

So they moved to Waterloo and turned it into the brass band Mecca of North America. The professor organized tattoos that attracted as many as seventy bands and 50,000 spectators to Waterloo Park at a time when the town's population was pushing 5,000. He founded Waterloo Music Company, which manufactured band instruments, many of which he gave to bandsmen who couldn't afford them. Thiele gave free music lessons, too, hence the title "Professor." He also bought land on which he built a summer camp for fledgling musicians, calling it Bandburg. Later Thiele was acclaimed as the father of Canadian brass band music.

Thirty years and countless accomplishments later, the Professor was awarded a day in his honour and paraded in an open convertible behind his band to Waterloo Park where thousands gathered to cheer. The driver of the convertible, Charlie Schneider, a close friend of Thiele's, told me about the event many years later.

"The Professor," Charlie said, "was sitting on top of the rear seat, waving to the crowd as we followed the band into Waterloo Park. When the band began to countermarch on the grass, I swung the car around them and headed towards the throng lining the field. I drove under some spruce trees without a thought as to how high the Professor was sitting. The crowd suddenly went quiet. I turned to see what the Professor might be doing and … he wasn't there. A spruce bough had swept him off. Right away a voice beside me hollered, 'Charlie, let me in!' It was the Professor, running beside the car. He was holding his hat in his hand. The back of his jacket was covered with grass stains. I stopped and opened the door, and in no time he was back on top of the rear seat, waving. The crowd went crazy. He always surprised them."

20

No Steroids for the Terriers

nfortunately, today's role models in professional baseball sustain their energy at manic levels by ingesting steroids, cocaine, Sudafed, and even Alka-Seltzer. These are called "performance-enhancing drugs." George Brown finds this disgusting and quite unnecessary.

"I knew some great athletes on the old Galt Terriers baseball club in the 1930s," George says, "and the only performance-enhancing drug they ingested was called 'beer,' and they never ingested it before or during a game, only after, usually on the bus." This might explain why some of their post-game performances exceeded anything they did on the playing field.

George Brown recounts the time that Dave Johnson, who claimed to be a pitcher, humiliated the team by bombing out in Hamilton. Johnson, who pitched the ball the way he did the dice, ran an illegal gambling den under a grocery store on Dickson Street right across the road from the Galt Police Station. He was so bad in Hamilton that when the Terriers returned to Galt they stopped the bus at Soper Park so that four of the players could throw him into the creek above the dam. They then drove off and left him to soak.

One time in St. Thomas the Terriers' coach, "Bush" McWhirter, who never used or needed performance-enhancing drugs at any time, got into such a row with the umpire that he was ordered off the field. He kept shouting from the stands, however, until two policemen carried him out of the park. The team, which had lost, picked him up at the courthouse on the way home.

On the bus McWhirter reviewed the game at the top of his lungs, ticking off all the umpire's bad calls and stolen-base tag-outs. The players, fired up by McWhirter and a case of beer, began to boast about how fast they could run. Before the bus reached Paris they were running the bases in the aisle. At the south end of the Paris main street, by the cenotaph, McWhirter ordered the bus to stop. He declared there would be a race to see who was the fastest man on the team. It was 8:00 p.m. on a hot Saturday, and the street was crowded with pedestrians. Because of the heat the players had stripped down to their shorts. Young George Brown, who was the Terriers' bat boy, was in constant fear that the whole team was about to be arrested, so he hid in the back of the bus.

"Eight or nine guys piled out," George said, "and when McWhirter hollered, 'Go,' they streaked through the traffic a full block to the Arlington Hotel with the bus in pursuit." As he recalls, George Heggie won the race. Boyd Shewan was a close second.

I can't imagine Boyd Shewan running up the Paris main street in his underwear, especially since he became my morally rematrixed drill sergeant principal at Central School in Galt and would lecture the boys against peeing behind the trees in the playground.

Before he married Marjorie Dykeman, George Brown settled down to run a cycle shop and developed into a tempestuous athlete on the ball field and ice rink. His goaltending on the ice might have landed him in the National Hockey League today. George says he brought his temper under control by learning to play the violin. His brother, Dave, a Galt firefighter, was musical, too, and sang so that he caused people to cry. George gave up the violin one night when he smashed it over a friend's head while watching a Toronto Maple Leafs–Boston Bruins hockey game on television. No telling when he'll give up beer.

Back in those golden days no one ever got arrested for running down main street in their underwear. Now you can get arrested for carrying a cream pie within 100 yards of the prime minister.

21

George Recalls Scott's Opera House

*W*hen George Brown's violin was in for repair, he found peace and diversion at Scott's Opera House. The flaking brown playbills of Scott's Opera House in the archives at Galt City Hall reveal there was indeed entertainment before television. Dated from 1903 to 1918, the playbills are loaded with famous stage names that make one swoon with nostalgia. Who can forget Mortimer Ellingham, Adelaide Eaton Colton, and Lonnie Lorrimer Deanne? And how about Mack Sennett, Bessie Smith, Billie Burke, and Sophie Tucker? Mack Sennett played a minor role in the musical comedy *Wang*, but later became Hollywood's king of slapstick and creator of the Keystone Kops.

George says he went to the movies whenever he wasn't playing hockey. He saw his first movie at Scott's. It was called *Wings*, not quite silent because a man behind the screen reproduced the sound of airplanes with a vacuum cleaner. George played goal in a tough inter-county league and once punched out Howie Meeker, which was directly responsible for Meeker's lifelong crusade against violence on the ice. But that's another story.

Maude Adams, the leading lady in American theatre, played Scott's in the role she immortalized in *Peter Pan*, flying over the audience suspended in a harness hooked to an intricate network of wires. Special effects rivalled anything you might see onstage today. After the performance of *Queen Zephra* in 1903, the stage was showered with 40,000 yards of serpentine confetti of every colour.

And there was suspense. A note in heavy type on the playbill of *That Imprudent Young Couple* warns: "Owing to the very unusual and unconventional ending of the third act, it is desirable that the audience remain seated until the descent of the curtain." Management didn't want a riot. The titles of many of the productions, not yet controversial in 1903, would surely cause homophobes to picket with bullhorns today: *The Gay Mr. Goldstein*, *The Gay Musician*, *The Fairies of Ireland*, *When Women Love*, and *Mutt and Jeff's Wedding*. Scott's was way ahead of its time.

Playbill advertisements for local businesses didn't waste words: "Smith Can Press Your Clothes Right." This ad appeared unchanged from 1903 to 1908 when Smith disappeared. The Imperial Hotel on Water Street rented rooms for $1.50 to $2 a day and offered "free sample rooms," possibly code for something that led to the hotel burning down.

Stage equipment suppliers advertised their wares, too. A note in the playbill for *Over Niagara Falls* in all versions A, B, and C reads: "Boats supplied by King Folding Canvas Boat Co. of Kalamazoo, Mich." Another ad reads: "Pistols used in *Within the Law* supplied by Maxim Silent Firearms Co. of Hartford, Conn." The whole back page of a 1904 playbill carries an invitation for anyone who can make it to the wedding of Mary Ellen Carruthers and James Robertson and the reception in Glen Morris, June 1, Wednesday at 1:00 p.m. For every performance of *Ten Nights in a Bar Room*, a lucky ticket holder won a ton of coal.

The variety of entertainment was unlimited. Right after the great Ed Hoyt (who can forget Ed?) did *Hamlet*, Joseph Sheehan, America's greatest tenor, starred in *Salome* with a cast of fifty. Next came the Tzigani Troupe of acrobats accompanied by "the world's greatest singing chorus." Clarence Bennett, as Native chief Tabywana in *The Squawman*, spoke entirely in the Ute language under the tutelage of Baco White of the Ute reservation. The audience, until informed of this, just thought he had a speech impediment. The renowned hypnotist Sevengala carried a special note in his program: "Persons who cannot be hypnotized ... idiots and lunatics (except in special cases), children under the age of three and persons under the influence of alcohol." It had to do with their attention span.

Local talent performed at Scott's, too. The YMCA annually staged a Grand Gymnastic Exhibition, including stunts on a real horse, a ladies' physical culture and Morris dancing demonstration, and Sebastapol playing on a guitar. The Dumfries Foundry Benefit Society held a concert and minstrel show after which A.E. Williams, year after year, played "The Death of Nelson" on the trombone.

A wealthy cattle drover named Scott built the opera house in 1889 because he believed the district could do with a bit of class. Scott made the ushers and orchestra members wear tuxedos and stiff white shirts, and every playbill carried the warning: "The by-law against spitting on the floor of any public building will be strictly enforced in this theatre."

22
The Daring Hespeler Girls

With the Great Depression ending and World War II looming, five girls who worked at Dominion Woollens in Hespeler decided to have a long-deserved fling. Ethel, Margaret, and Isabella Wilson, daughters of the chief of police, and the Prestwick sisters, Agnes and Nel, had saved $70 each and decided to blow it on two weeks in New York. It was Ethel Wilson's idea.

Train fare was too expensive, so Ethel did the logical thing. She phoned Hespeler's only taxi driver, Allan Leonard, and asked what the fee to take five girls to New York for two weeks would be. He said he would have to think it over because he had been married less than a month and didn't know how his bride would react to his running off to New York with a carload of girls. Besides, the town would have no taxi service while he was away. Allan called back in fifteen minutes. Sure, he would do it. The fee? How about $60? No, not each, but for all five.

So off they went, three girls in the back seat and two in the front, with Leonard and luggage piled so there was just room enough to see out the windshield. It was so hot that the girls took off their stockings and hung them out the windows to air. They drove to New York non-stop, the only respite being a baseball game with American custom officers at the Roosevelt Bridge east of Brockville. The game ended when one of the girls batted the ball into the St. Lawrence River.

New York opened its small-town heart to the girls. At the St. James Hotel where they stayed the desk clerk and resident guests were like parents, advising them where it was safe to go. They got one large room on an upper floor with five cots. There was a great view, and the girls took turns sleeping on the cot next to the window. Allan Leonard slept at the YMCA.

The improbable kept happening. A Hespelerite, Charles Panabaker, then living in New York, chanced upon the girls on the street and took it upon himself to show them all the sights they had seen on postcards: the Empire State Building, the Statue of Liberty, Radio City Music Hall and, best of all, the New York World's Fair, where they saw such wonders as the first television sets and the latest developments in steam locomotives. It was at Radio City Music Hall that Isabella Wilson fell under the spell of showbiz. She later returned to star on the Broadway stage.

The girls all carried their money in little pouches on strings around their necks, dangling them down to hide in their brassieres where, according to Leonard, there was ample storage space. As their money drained away, they began to eat from vending machines at the Automat. But before leaving for home they decided to blow the bundle on one last meal in a good restaurant. They searched about and somehow wound up at a second-floor banquet hall featuring a splendid buffet. Gracious hostesses invited them to help themselves to all they might want. After unleashing their pent-up appetites, they began to worry about the bill. But there was no bill. They had wandered into a convention hall, and the staff thought they must be representatives of the sponsoring corporation.

The girls' money did run out on the way home, and their peerless driver, Allan Leonard, had to pay for their meals out of his taxi fare. He stopped at a vineyard in upstate New York and bought a gallon jug of grape juice that was on sale. Because the girls had brought back a lot of boxes in addition to their luggage, the only room left for the jug was on the floor between Leonard's knees. On a bumpy road near the border the top on the jug blew off and Leonard got drenched. How a cab driver drenched in grape juice travelling with five hysterical girls got through customs is a mystery.

Back in Hespeler, Leonard had to recount his adventure to everyone he met on the street and in his cab. Dr. Henderson, his dentist, asked him every time he went to have his teeth fixed. "Tell me again,

Allan, about the trip to New York," the doctor would say. He must have had a plausible story for his wife, because his marriage survived.

Ethel, like her stage-struck sister, Isabella, returned to New York but in a more conventional role to work for the publisher Collier Macmillan. Later she returned to Hespeler to be the company's office manager for twenty-five years.

23

Isabella Wilson

Isabella Wilson, stage-struck during her trip to New York, returned and landed a job with the British Trade Ministry. This lasted only until she auditioned and got a job singing at the Roxy Theatre. She had a great contralto voice nourished in Hespeler's St. Andrew's Church Choir and the Galt Choral Society. Her voice teacher, Urquhart Ireland, was the chemist at Dominion Woollens. Everyone in town, it seemed, worked there.

At the Roxy she shared the stage with Louis Armstrong, and before long was singing five and six hours a day at Radio City Music Hall. Next she progressed to chorus and leading roles at the famous Paper Mill Playhouse in Millburn, New Jersey. World War II now well under-way, she went on a long stint with the USO show, entertaining troops in Africa, Egypt, India, and Burma. Isabella was awarded the honorary rank of captain and became close friends with Ed Wynn and Phil Silvers.

After the war, it was back to the Paper Mill Playhouse. Soon she made the big leap to Broadway and landed a role in *Up in Central Park*, a Michael Todd production featuring Noah Beery, brother of famed gravel-voiced movie actor Wallace Beery. Next she auditioned for two blockbuster productions: *Yours Is My Heart*, starring world-renowned tenor Richard Tauber, and *South Pacific* with Enzio Pinza. She was accepted by both productions and had to make a choice. For advice she turned to her voice teacher, Wellington Smith, sister of opera superstar Lily Pons. These people, we might note, never worked at Dominion Woollens. Wellington Smith told her there was really no choice but to go with Richard Tauber, even though he was a notorious bottom pincher, because who had ever heard of Enzio Pinza? So she joined the cast of *Yours Is My Heart*. That show played only a few months on Broadway; *South Pacific* lasted more than twenty years.

As much as she loved Broadway, Isabella always said that when she died she wanted to come home and be buried in Hespeler. During the peak of her career at age thirty-eight, she developed a brain tumor and died at home during a chance visit. Married at thirty-two, widowed at thirty-four, dead at thirty-eight.

24

More About Hespeler

We never seem to run out of Hespeler stories. Possibly because Hespelerites have better-than-average memories. Maybe it's something in their drinking water. They remember their town's past the way the rest of us remember our families' past, and like a family, they take care of one another.

Back in the Hungry Thirties, during the Great Depression, Gordon Klager, president and general manager of Dominion Woollens and Worsteds, decided that if Hespeler was to survive those terrible times his plant should employ at least one member of every family in town. He succeeded in finding jobs for two-thirds of the working population.

The town clerk, Winfield Brewster, seemed in the 1930s to hold the mortgages on nearly everyone's house, but he never foreclosed on anyone. Whenever someone couldn't pay, he would ask, "What's the hurry?"

And Hespelerites fondly remember old town characters: Professor Jenner, who played the town's first pipe organ, had a passion for rhubarb and conducted the choir while inebriated; Emma Lawson, the savant who memorized everyone's post office box combination and enlivened the main street by breaking wind like a tuba; Buck Salisbury, always in trouble, who set fire to his straw jail cell mattress and himself and had to be extinguished by the volunteer fire department; and, of course, Chief Tom Wilson, who kept a semblance of law and order with no police cruiser for more than forty years.

Gord Klager was always testing Chief Tom on points of law. On Fridays, payday at Dominion Woollens, Mr. Klager, the chief, and a special deputy sworn in for the day would climb into Gord's Model T Ford to drive the $12,000 payroll from the bank to the plant. They all sported revolvers. One day Gord removed the ring off the car's steering wheel and began to steer only with spokes.

"You can't do that," Chief Tom said. "It's against the law."

Gord then challenged the chief to find anything in the Highway Traffic Act that said he couldn't steer with spokes.

When the chief, who always carried a copy of the act with him, couldn't find anything, he said, "One of these days, Gord, I'm going to get you."

The chief was also the noxious weed inspector and was always bursting into Gord's office with a fistful of deadly weeds he had uprooted on Dominion Woollen property. Gord would get out his weed identification book, which he always kept in his desk drawer, and prove the chief wrong, and again the chief would say, "One of these days, Gord, I'm going to get you." He never did.

Much as they hated to, Hespelerites sometimes had to leave town. Reg Prior, nineteen years old in 1928, was earning 12 cents an hour making washing machines when his uncle offered him 53 cents an hour to work in the nickel mines in Sudbury. His uncle was a foreman there. The whole family was so eager to get Reg up there that his grandmother washed his pants with his train ticket in the back pocket. Reg sent money home from the mine to help support his family for several years. He found cause to come home just in time to help the Petrinka brothers haul a ten-foot-high metal cross up the Lutheran Church steeple and bolt it to the top. "What a view of the town I had from up there," Reg said.

He got a job working for the Jardine brothers. They ran a renowned machine tool plant that shipped parts all over the world. Wally Jardine, the plant manager, was a perfectionist. He was also short on patience. One day, when everything didn't go right in the carpentry department where Reg worked, Wally got so mad that he hurled his claw hammer through a window. It wasn't open. The hammer landed in the middle of Highway 24. Wally ran out and, dodging the traffic, picked it up and pitched it back into the plant through another window. The men in the carpentry shop, wise enough not to snicker, stood smartly at attention when Wally charged back in. "Don't just stand there!" he hollered. "Get me two more windows."

One story leads to another. Chief Tom Wilson lived with his family in a house below Tannery Street on a hill so steep that a man attending a party near the top slid down after an ice storm and couldn't make it back up to retrieve his hat. But that isn't today's story.

One of the chief's daughters, Ethel Gibson (now deceased), recounted to me that one warm summer night in the 1940s she and her mother were startled by screaming in front of the house. They ran out to find a girl, about twelve years old, crouched over a middle-aged woman lying on the sidewalk unconscious. "It's my mother!" the girl screamed. "She's dying! Get the priest!" Ethel and her mother carried the woman into their living room, laid her out on some blankets, and put a pillow under her head. "Please hurry," the girl said. "There's no time to spare. Get the priest." She was hysterical, and Ethel's mother, caught up in the panic, phoned the priest before she called the doctor. And the priest or the doctor or possibly the telephone switchboard operator, also swept along by the drama, called the undertaker.

They all arrived at the same time. The priest, Father Ford, apologized right off for the alcohol on his breath. He was fighting a cold, he said, and was taking a little something for it. Dr. Hutchinson arrived in a car driven by his son. The doctor, too, was fighting a cold and had taken sufficient medicinal whiskey that he didn't feel steady enough to drive himself to the home of the chief of police regardless of the emergency. The undertaker, Charley Stager, kept his breath to himself and sat quietly in the kitchen while Dr. Hutchinson ministered to the woman and Father Ford got ready for action. The smell of alcohol was so strong, Ethel said, that no one could tell if the woman also had any on her breath.

Out came the smelling salts, the woman revived, and the Last Rites were shelved. Charley Stager called a cab to take the woman and her daughter home because he didn't want to deliver them in his mortuary pickup. Oddly, no one bothered to ask the woman her name and address and what might have been troubling her. She must have survived, though, because she was seen walking the streets of Hespeler for years afterwards.

Here's an account of how two veterans of the Boer War met by chance in Hespeler. First we must consider that many people have never heard of the Boer War. It was fought in South Africa from 1899 to 1902 to enable the British to take the diamond mines away from the Dutch-descended Afrikaners. Winston Churchill became a hero in the process. British casualties totalled 28,000 men dead or missing. The Afrikaners, who were better at ducking, lost only 4,000 troops, but an additional 20,000 women and children died of disease in British concentration camps. "But what good of it at last?" quoth little Peterkin. "Why that I cannot say," said father. "But 'twas a famous victory." More than 8,000 Canadian volunteers fought for the British. Nearly 300 were killed in combat and by disease and 252 were wounded. Most men went to fight not because of patriotic fervour but for want of adventure. When they returned to Canada, they lost track of one another and reunited usually by chance.

Bert Brown of Hespeler had a father, Leonard Brown, in the Boer War, a cavalry officer in the British Shropshire Highland Light Infantry that took part in the relief of Mafeking, a victory that should be drilled into the mind of every schoolboy today. Leonard Brown was wounded in the battle by a bullet that passed through his leg and killed his horse. In 1911 he immigrated to Canada, got married in Brandon, Manitoba, in 1912, and landed in Hespeler, where little Bert was born in 1920.

One day in the mid-1920s Bert's mother went to Prong's Bookstore to buy him some books for school. She was in a hurry and opened the door with such gusto that it smacked into a man behind it and knocked his hat off. He was Tom Wilson, chief of police. Testy after a nasty knock on the head and his loss of dignity, the chief hollered that he had a mind to charge her with assaulting an officer. She shrieked back that he should have seen her coming and had the common decency to open the door for a lady.

The row escalated so that the chief, patting the handcuffs in his back pocket, threatened to arrest her on the spot. However, better judgment cautioned him against the spectacle of dragging off a young woman in handcuffs for knocking off his hat. So the chief mopped his brow and suggested that Mrs. Brown and her husband drop down to the station the next night when cooler heads presided and talk the matter over. To this she agreed, but the next night, fearing she might start shrieking again, she sent her husband, Leonard, alone.

Upon entering the chief's office, Leonard immediately spotted a Boer War memorial plaque on the wall. The chief, it turned out, had fought in a brigade beside the troop that Leonard had fought in. This put the Battle of Prong's Bookstore on the back burner. Over a bottle of rye that the chief reserved for special occasions, the two relived the Boer War for three hours. The Battle of Prong's Bookstore got only a passing mention and an apology from the chief. After Leonard lurched home with rye on his breath, his wife demanded, "Where the hell have you been?" And she started a row that stopped only when they both feared the neighbours might call Chief Wilson.

Getting back to the Boer War, I should mention that the Boer troops wore tight round hats under which they usually stored a derringer. Upon disarming a Boer prisoner one day, Leonard Brown found under the hat not a pistol but a Bible. This he brought home as a souvenir along with a two-foot-long stuffed baby crocodile. When he died, the Bible, at Leonard's request, was buried with him … just in case he had a reunion with a Boer somewhere.

Bill Okrafka and two brothers who owned a trucking company got the job of moving the old Hespeler Catholic cemetery to a new location, and in the process they dug up a Boer War veteran in full dress uniform. "He tumbled out of a casket we were moving," said Bill, holding his nose. The moving was a nauseating and somewhat spooky job that continued on and off for thirty years.

George Woods, who chauffeured Chief Wilson from crime to crime, was called on to taxi some dignitaries to the official closing of the cemetery and told this story. The Catholic cemetery, behind the old public school on Kribs Street, had become full and neglected. This was more than eighty years ago. Groundhogs burrowed there and scattered human bones around their mounds. Children from the school played in the cemetery and proudly brought the bones, which they fancied belonged to Natives, home to their parents. Their parents, suspecting the worst, turned the bones over to the local priest, who collected them in a shoe-box. The time had come, he decided, for the cemetery to be closed. Not only closed but moved, bodies and all, to less-disturbed ground in the New Hope (but don't count on it) Cemetery on Cooper Street. That was the job that fell to the Okrafka brothers.

The town clerk, Winfield Brewster, the man who wouldn't fore-close on anyone's mortgage, decided that the moving of the cemetery should be done with dignity and unction and so mustered the mayor, members of the town council and the cemetery board, and local and county health officers and marched them up to Kribs Street for the spe-cial service. They were joined there by the parish priest and regional bishop. Following pertinent prayers and incantations, the bishop, with a pass of his hand in the air, proclaimed with great solemnity, "I now declare this cemetery closed." Everyone then donned their hats and rode up to the New Hope Cemetery. There, after more prayers, the shoebox full of human bones was lowered into a standard cavernous pit dug for the occasion. It was assumed that only Catholic bones were consecrated there, but you know what kids bring home. There might have been the odd piece of groundhog, or worse, Protestant.

After the shoebox was covered with earth, Mr. Brewster invited the dignitaries back to his office in the town hall to sign the required affidavits and polish off a bottle of rye. According to Mr. Woods, even the teetotalers, out of a sense of civic duty, joined in toasts to the new cemetery and the memory of the old. Soon what had been a dreary affair became a joyous event, and there was talk of closing cemeteries and opening new ones all over the place.

Mr. Woods, the founder of Woods Transport, recalled stories about his father, William Woods, who delivered freight around Hespeler with a horse and rig. One day he picked up a large roll of linoleum from the railway freight sheds and delivered it to Stager's Furniture Store on

Queen Street. The roll weighed hundreds of pounds and had to be rolled down skids to the walk in front of the store. Mr. Stager looked at the serial number on the roll and said it was the wrong one and that it had to be returned. So Mr. Woods recruited all the store assistants and every able-bodied passerby to haul the roll back up the skids and onto the cart.

Midway through this formidable task, Emma Lawson, the savant who memorized everyone's post box combination, chanced by and urged the men to greater efforts by shouting, "Heave, push, heave!" She had such enthusiasm that she had to pitch in. However, just as the men had the roll to the top of the skids, Emma, as was her wont, let loose a tremendous fart. This action took the wind out of the men, too, and they collapsed in fits of laughter and let the linoleum roll back to the sidewalk. Emma didn't appreciate the laughter and stalked away, scoffing loudly about men with weak brains. The next effort to shoulder the roll back up the skids failed, as well, when one of the men emulated Emma's performance. However, they did, finally, succeed.

There is only one Hespeler in the whole world. There are six Galts in the United States alone and at least eighteen Prestons that we know of. Cambridges and Blairs clutter maps everywhere. Perhaps that's why these towns seldom attempt reunions. No one would know which town to go to.

25
A Scare for Hitler

In 1939, on the brink of World War II, displays of military might were popular and air shows were favourites. Brantford hosted an air show one Saturday afternoon in August of that year, and my father drove the family down to see it. The Brantford aerodrome was in a meadow fenced in to keep neighbouring cows out, just north of what is now the Highway 403 overpass.

A good part of the show consisted of Tiger Moths doing wobbly loops and buzzing a couple of dilapidated hangars, but the feature attraction was a fly-past of a dozen U.S. Army Air Corps fighter planes from Buffalo. They flew past because they were forbidden to land on grass.

A hush fell after all civilian planes circling the field had been shooed away. Then what we had held our breath for arrived with a frightening roar as a dozen brown monoplanes skimmed over the treetops from the south. (U.S. Air Force planes were at that time brown because the flyboys were still a branch of the army.) Back and forth the pilots roared at more than 200 miles per hour, gunning their engines to put fear into the hearts of the enemy and tears in our eyes.

"Those are called monoplanes," my dad said. "Biplanes are all washed up." Then he huffed and said, "I just wish Hitler could see this," blissfully unaware that a German pilot had just set the world air speed record of 469 miles per hour in a souped-up Messerschmitt.

War brought a new morality, and we began to watch airplanes on Sundays. One week we would be at Malton Airport, now Pearson International, and the next week we would be at Burford Military Field, the Commonwealth Air Training Plan base celebrated by Don Harron in his World War II memoir *Terror in the Skies over London, Paris, and Brantford.*

We visited Malton Airport only if my dad had managed to get enough gas ration stamps from Jack Dickens. The Malton terminal (free parking on the grass) was a long two-storey white clapboard building full of manual typewriters. A corridor through its centre led to a second two-storey white clapboard building sporting a rooftop observation deck over the departure lounge. You had to pay 10 cents at a turnstile before you could ascend the stairs and stand in the sun or rain on the observation deck, and there was usually a small crowd of people who wouldn't risk the dime until they were assured by an authority that a plane was about to land or take off. When that happened, the surging crowd spun the turnstile so that it slapped men in their crotches and ladies on their behinds and flung children in all directions. Children got in free.

Trans-Canada Airlines, Air Canada's predecessor, then flew Lockheed Lodestars, matronly machines with two engines and twin tails that could safely carry two dozen passengers for short hops at altitudes not requiring oxygen. Passengers, still high on the novelty of air travel, affected dignity and importance while walking the 100 feet from the terminal to the plane, not easy while carrying their own luggage. Sometimes they waved from atop the three steps leading up to the rear passenger door, and sometimes they bumped their heads.

We became obsessed with watching planes. A TCA flight from London to Malton passed low over Galt at 4:00 p.m. each day, and we ran into the yard at the sound of its approach. Boys in the street would holler, "It's a Stuka dive bomber!" and we had to look to make sure it wasn't.

Burford Airfield, nowhere near the town of Burford and now the real Brantford Airport, became our favourite Sunday afternoon watch. We parked our car with dozens of others on a gravel road beside the field and ate Spam sandwiches while watching yellow twin-engine Avro Ansons take off and land nose to tail. "I just wish Hitler could see this," my dad would say. Burford was a training base for bomber crews, and they flew over Galt for five years, a never-ending drone day and night. The night sky winked with red and green navigation lights. At last we got bored and quit looking up in the sky. Over in Europe it was another matter.

26
All Aboard to See
Their Majesties

On June 6, 1939, 800 public schoolchildren marched from their schools in Galt down to George Street to board a passenger train. We were off to Kitchener to see the king and queen, George VI and Elizabeth, who were touring the dominion to redeem the Royal Family after Edward VIII ran off with an American divorcee and had tea with Adolf Hitler.

It challenges the imagination to see a passenger train on George Street, fourteen olive-green coaches pulled by two ancient steam engines, stretching from Dickson Park to Queen's Square, but I see it on my mental screen now. The little steam engines, built before 1910, were all the creaky trestles on the back Kitchener line could shoulder and looked as if at night they might shelter under large tea cozies.

The rail line, nostalgically referred to as the "Old Dutch Mail," normally shunted a couple of cars of coal to factories at the south end of George Street twice a week. A century earlier it had carried the cholera plague from Kitchener to Galt in the gullets of a troop of entertainers. Now was its final moment of glory.

We kids, girded with peanut-butter-and-jam sandwiches, were ecstatic. For many of us it was our first train ride. It was mine. And to be dispatched this way to see the king and queen on a school day (June 6 was a Tuesday in 1939) was exhilarating beyond control. George Street crawled with kids who looked as if they had just been hit over the head, turning round and round as they walked, herded by crazed schoolteachers trying to get them into their assigned coaches.

At last it was "All aboard" and one of the little engines tooted its whistle. Our coach gave a lurch.

"We're moving!" we all shouted as we chuffed past Reid's Lumber Yard and Dickson Park up a stiff grade where the George Street extension runs now. The train wasn't allowed any more than eight miles per hour on that thin rail. The day was hot, so the coach windows were open and we bathed in wisps of bituminous smoke, steam, and valve oil.

We sang "You Can't Go to Heaven on Roller Skates" and "The Quartermaster's Store," and every time we came to a crossing or village, such as Blair, where crowds had gathered to cheer us on and anxious parents watched to see if anyone had fallen off, we sang ourselves hoarse. By the time we threaded over the back streets of Kitchener, we were squeaking like mice.

Our train stopped at the Canadian National Railways main line, and we disembarked to stand beside the track half a mile west of Kitchener station where the official reception was to take place. For two hours we stood in the blazing sun, tired and dizzy with the heat. Some of us fainted, and cold compresses appeared.

The green-and-gold pilot train that always preceded the royal train to make sure the track was safe roared by and we cheered wildly. We realized we had cheered the wrong train when the blue-and-gold cowl of the royal train proper presented itself at the station.

Crackles of speeches drifted on the wind, and a band struck up. At last the real train headed our way and accelerated past in a blizzard of smoke and cinders. The king and queen were still on the observation platform of the last coach, and we saw them for perhaps four seconds. They were waving. Rob Brown, who was looking at Margaret Ruddell, didn't even see the train. For the next hour and a half we backed down to George Street in our own train, too hot and tired to sing, just picking our noses and savouring our moment in history.

The next day the schoolchildren of Paris got their royal treat. Paris wasn't on the royal agenda, but the train, returning to Toronto from London, had to stop there for coal and water. Alerted to this, officials hastily erected a pavilion for the mayor, councillors, political bagmen, and clergy at the spot were the royal observation car would stop. This had been determined by precise measurements of the train's length obtained by the Member of Parliament for Brant County from the Royal Canadian Mounted Police. But this day two coaches had been inexplicably removed from the train so that when it nosed up to the coaling tower the coach carrying their majesties stopped 160 feet past the viewing stand. The crowd, which wasn't to be allowed near the royal coach, broke and ran after it, leaving the dignitaries marooned on their pavilion, speeches in hand, the flower girl in tears while the town band played "God Save the King" out of tune. The king and queen, chatting with the crowd, clearly enjoyed this.

The following day the queen officially opened a four-lane highway named after her and pulled a switch that turned on overhead lights on the only fully illuminated freeway in North America ... from Toronto to Niagara Falls. The lights stayed on for two months but went out when World War II was declared, never to come on again.

27
Pop, What's a Gentile?

I remember September 3, 1939, vividly, because that was the day I learned I was a Gentile. It was also the day England declared war on Germany. I was at Bronte Creek Provincial Park, west of Oakville, celebrating Labour Day with my sister, Shirley, and parents and Bill and Emily Jeffs, who kept a trailer there. The men went to Bronte to fish and the women to feed them. The kids could swim in Lake Ontario. There was a decent little beach where men were compelled by law to wear bathing suits with tops. Topless men were ordered to cover up or leave. It was a comfortable place to hear war break out.

We gathered around the radio. Adolf Hitler was going berserk, and Britain's prime minister, Neville Chamberlain, was droning on about "enough is enough." My dad and Bill Jeffs had both fought in the first war to end all wars and were eager to get back into this one. Pop wanted to return to France just to defend the Vimy Ridge Memorial. Mom was willing to let him go, but said she was glad I was only nine and too young to sign up. I agreed.

I wandered away from the radio to play war games with my balsa wood glider and soon found myself up by the park gate. The gatekeeper was turning away an old Essex touring car occupied by a couple with a lot of kids. The couple looked distraught, and the kids looked scared as they backed out. "Sorry, full up," the gatekeeper had told them, and immediately let in the next car. I sensed that this strange transaction was somehow related to a sign at the gate that said Gentiles Only.

The *Canadian Oxford Dictionary* defines *Gentile* as "a person who is not Jewish," and also as "non-Mormon." I didn't have a dictionary at hand, so I asked my dad, "Pop, what's a Gentile?"

"That's us," he said. "Why do you ask?"

I told him about the sign at the gate and the people turned away. "How does the gatekeeper know who are Gentiles?" I asked.

"He doesn't," Pop said. "He just turns away everyone in old cars. That keeps out most of the Jews."

I gathered that included Albert Einstein, Benny Goodman, Jack Benny, and Jesus, provided they didn't turn up in limousines. How we got by in our 1929 Chevrolet I'll never know. When I told Pop how upset the people turned away looked, he said that it was a damn shame but that there was nothing we could do because the law was the law.

"Gentiles only" really was the law then for any legal body that wished to pass it. The council of Port Elgin was then debating a law that would prohibit Jews from owning any property in town.

Pop and Bill Jeffs got onto the German people for allowing such a nut bar as Hitler to take over. "Why didn't they stop him as soon as they saw him shooting people who were trying to stop him?" Pop asked.

Soon they were trying to figure out a way to keep Germans out of the park. Emily Jeffs was so disturbed by Hitler on the radio that she couldn't remember eating the pork chop she had just fried on the camp stove.

I don't know how long the Gentiles Only sign stayed there. No one mentioned it when we drove past it on our way home.

28

The Palace and Jane Russell

A lot of kids in Galt in 1939 were unaware that World War II was declared on September 3, because the Palace Theatre staged its grand opening on September 2 and we could think of nothing else. It started with a Saturday matinee featuring two westerns and the worst vaudeville (live) since Rosy Devlin's horse, Ralph, jumped into the orchestra pit at Scott's Opera House. A comedian in baggy pants, a sort of forerunner of Rodney Dangerfield, told a long, long story about his spendthrift wife who bought a dress with 153 buttons up the front and 153 button up the back while he had to hold his pants up with a nail. We shrieked with laughter.

To upstage the other two cinemas in town, the Capitol and the Grand, the Palace offered the ladies a sixty-nine-piece dinnerware set free, one piece at a time, provided they attended one movie a week for sixty-nine weeks. The dinner plates alone, the ads boasted, were worth more than the adult price of admission — 20 cents. Children got in for 10 cents. Special Sunday midnight shows allowed smoking and promoted petting. There were no westerns, but there were plenty of G-men with machine guns mowing down gangsters. This was when J. Edgar Hoover was wearing his first dress.

Before the midnight shows a street preacher wrote apocalyptic forebodings on the pavement with coloured chalk and railed against whoever was on the illuminated marquee, even if it was Hopalong Cassidy. Too bad the preacher wasn't still around in 1949 when the Palace screened *The Outlaw* starring the two and only Jane Russell, then a 44D cup.

The movie was produced by Howard Hughes in 1943 but was barred from release by the Hayes censorship office for six years. The Palace got *The Outlaw* because Galt's premier theatre, the Capitol, turned it down. The Capitol hosted only uplifting family movies such as *Gone with the Wind*. My dad, who had forbidden me to read the novel *Gone with the Wind* because he had heard it was a bit smutty, said, "Don't let me catch you in that lineup for *The Outlaw*." I promised. My friend Len Iseler said that his dad, a Lutheran minister, had also made him promise not to go. So the two of us had to sneak through the 7:00 p.m. lineup shielding our faces with newspapers.

The Outlaw certainly lived up to its billing. It was almost as lurid as some of the bath oil commercials shown today on prime-time television. The hottest scene was when Jane Russell wrestled with an outlaw in a hayloft. There was cleavage flying right, left, and centre and close-ups of straw undulating to stertorous breathing.

I came out in time to see my dad and Uncle Bill Spring in the 9:00 p.m. lineup. Pop went rigid when he spotted me and called me over. "Now don't go blabbing this to your mother." I didn't have to. Uncle Billy blabbed it to my mother. Later, at home, I overheard her asking Pop in her prosecutor's voice what the movie was like. "Disgusting," Pop said. "I don't know how they get away with it."

The Palace folded in 1959. Jane Russell defied gravity until 1970 when she retired from films, got religion, and made an honest living doing brassiere commercials for "the well-endowed woman."

29

The Great School Concerts

*B*ack in the 1940s there was only one thing that Galt Public School pupils enjoyed more than the end of the school year and that was Bill McFadyen's annual massed choir concert in Dickson Park. Mr. McFadyen, the music master of Galt's elementary schools, conceived the project and undertook to train, orchestrate, and conduct all the pupils from Central, Manchester, Dickson, St. Andrews, and St. Mary's in one huge choir, an undertaking that each year brought him to the brink of physical and nervous exhaustion. Friends were always concerned about his health, but he told them, "These concerts won't kill me. I live for them."

The kids loved the concerts. So did their parents. So did everyone without kids. And so did thousands of spectators from out of town who drove in to listen.

The choir had three-part harmony, and the children had to be trained to sing their harmony lines separately while Mr. McFadyen hummed the melody or played it on his tiny mobile pump organ. Whole schools sang different harmony lines. Each school got to rehearse en masse in its own schoolyard when the weather warmed up in May and June, but there was no provision for a dress rehearsal with all the schools. No one heard them harmonize until the night of the concert.

I recall a schoolyard rehearsal at Central in June 1940. The blitzkrieg had flattened France, and the Battle of Britain had just begun. The news was shocking and we were all scared. Mr. McFadyen, conducting from the landing at the school's front door, sounded the key on his mobile pump organ and launched us into "Land of Hope and Glory." We sang as if we were in tears. He raised his hand and stopped us. "Boys and girls," he said, "I know the news is not good, but we aren't quitters, are we? If we sing as if we are going to win, we will win." And he repeated emphatically, "We will win." So we sang just for him and we sang like angels (even Grenfell Davenport) and when we finished we heard applause from everyone who happened to be walking up and down Central School Hill.

The great concert was preceded by a great parade, and how we loved that! Each school formed platoons in its playground and marched behind its teachers and banners to the market square. There we were assigned various bands to lead us to the park. When a school learned it was to get the Galt Kiltie Band, a cheer went up. Everybody wanted the Kiltie Band because of its splendid red tunics and towering black busbies. Who cared if the outfits reeked of mothballs? The Kiltie Band was powered by big George Steep, who hammered his forty-five-pound symphony bass drum so that it sounded like a howitzer. No one wanted to march behind the Salvation Army Band with its dark uniforms and soft bass drum. The Salvation Army played gently as if it wanted to make peace with the enemy. Mr. McFadyen led the HLI Band, which also accompanied the massed choir in the park. He had to rewrite all the band's scores to accommodate the high pitch of the children's voices.

The Dickson Park grandstand seats were all marked out with chalk to squeeze in 1,580 boys and girls — eleven inches for the small ones, twelve inches for medium, and thirteen inches for the big kids. The precision of the seating was critical, because at one part in the program we were to hold overhead large coloured cards that formed a Union Jack.

We didn't sing just patriotic songs, but also popular numbers such as "Jeannie with the Light Brown Hair" and "Swanee River." The topper, of course, was "Land of Hope and Glory," and that was when we held the coloured cards over our heads to form the Union Jack. I didn't realize until I had my card aloft that I was holding out the white side instead of the red — a white spot right in the middle of the cross of St. George.

When we finished, the crowd went crazy, cheering and honking their car horns. The kids in the grandstand stood, proud as hell, many with faces streaming with tears, and cheered and waved back. Mr. McFadyen, drained but smiling, took his bows from his high wooden podium. He bowed to the crowd and set off more car horns. Next he bowed to the band. And then he bowed to the kids in the stands, and we cheered and clapped until our hands hurt.

After I found my parents and we chugged in our car through the dust of the traffic jam towards the gate, my dad said, "I just wish Hitler could have seen this. And that flag! How on earth did the kids get it right?" He was always amazed when kids got anything right. "It wasn't perfect, of course. Some kid, right in the middle of the cross of St. George, held up a white card instead of a red. Where were you sitting, anyway?"

30

My Flying Father

On the sparkling Christmas morning of 1942, my father decided he and I should mount a route-march out Cheese Factory Road and cook our breakfast on a campfire in the shelter of the pines. We tucked a parcel of bacon and eggs and a thermos of tea under the curl of a twelve-foot toboggan that we borrowed from the McNaught sisters on Concession Street and set off from the end of Lowrey Avenue, then only a block from our house, down Foster's Lane.

A foot of windblown snow had fallen overnight, and now the sun was gleaming on it and making us squint. The air was crisp and invigorating. Pop, at forty-five still as strong as a tractor, pulled the toboggan as if it were a feather. I was twelve and on skis and led the way. Pop called it a route-march because World War II was at its raging peak and he had reverted to the terminology of World War I in which he had fought.

We passed Myers Road and headed up Hill 60, named after a hill in France fought over by the Canadians and Germans in 1917 and on which Pop had fired off hundreds of rounds from his Lee-Enfield rifle, one of whose progenitors, James Paris Lee, had lived for a time in Galt.

"This is nothing compared with the real Hill 60," Pop said. "It was three times higher and we had to charge up it with forty pounds on our backs while being raked by enemy machine guns. The snow was twice as deep, too, the sun couldn't penetrate the gun smoke, and it was so cold we had to keep firing our rifles just so they wouldn't freeze tight."

Pop had a way of making me feel insignificant. In the summer, if we had a particularly violent thunderstorm and I said it was the loudest I had ever heard, he would return to the battlefield and say the storm reminded him of the calm between artillery barrages at Vimy Ridge. Every awesome experience I had paled before the onslaught of his photographic imagination.

We reached the bald peak of Hill 60 to the west of Cheese Factory Road, and Pop suggested I ski down to a knoll of evergreens and tell him if it was safe to follow on the toboggan. The descent was steep and fast enough to make my eyes water. Near the bottom I arrived at the lip of an enormous drift and managed to veer just in time to skid down its side. I scouted the foot of the drift and sank into three feet of freshly blown fluff.

From the hilltop Pop hollered, "All clear?" It echoed *"All clear ... clear ... clear?"*

Without a thought I hollered back, "All clear ... clear ... clear." I could hardly believe what I had done.

Standing to one side, I waited for Pop to heave into view. He appeared, plunging at a frightening speed with a big smile on his face. The smile switched to terror the moment he saw the abyss before him. Over he went, in slow motion as I recall, and disappeared in an explosion of silver fluff below. *Allah be praised*, I thought, years ahead of my time.

Only the rear of the toboggan stuck up above the snow, but soon the snow at the front end began to stir and Pop's head appeared. The space between the peak of his cap and his chin was a solid wedge of white. For lack of anything sensible to say I said, "Bet you've never seen a drift this high before."

A chunk of snow over his mouth broke away and he shouted, "You stupid ass ... *ass ... ass!* "That's the stupidest thing I've seen in my whole life ... *life ... life.*" He and the echoes kept this up until I was convinced I had topped all his record phenomena, that I now held the record for stupidity.

The toboggan, when we dug it out, was intact and not a single egg aboard had cracked. Pop, too, was intact, though I feared at any moment I wouldn't be. We cooked our breakfast under the pines, and it was so delicious that all was forgiven.

How many boys today, cursed by global warming, could find a ten-foot cliff of snow to send their fathers over? Pity.

31
Largo for Little Theatre

*B*ack in the 1940s the Galt Little Theatre and the Kiwanis Boys' Band both rehearsed in the old Gore Building on Main Street in adjacent rooms and on the same nights. They fought constantly. I played snare drum in the Boys' Band and recall one of its altercations vividly. Dick Ellis was bandmaster. He was a man of infinite patience and a virtuoso on the police whistle. Every time the band faltered in rehearsal, he would blow that great whistle and say, "Take it again from the top, boys." He loved that whistle. He could blow it until his neck was as thick as his head, and so loud that sometimes you would hear cars screech to a stop in the street below.

Anyway, this night we were rehearsing John Philip Sousa's "The Thunderer," a stirring and deafening march. Next door the Little Theatre was rehearsing something equally stirring, and between whistles we could hear the actors shouting through the walls. Presently there was a knock on the door and a tall paunchy man with rosy powder on his cheeks stepped in.

"Gentlemen," he said in a plummy British tone, "my name is John Kersh and I appreciate martial music, but if you care to take a break, I'll buy you all a pop." He punctuated his remarks with a silver wooden sword, then went on to explain that next door, Audrey Vale, one of Canada's finest actresses, was rehearsing a scene that required her to weep and she couldn't quite make it during "The Thunderer."

"Not to worry," Dick said, pulling out "Operatic Echoes," a score he said was easy to weep to. "Take it from the largo, boys, and keep it down." And he blew his whistle.

"Operatic Echoes" didn't go over next door, either, and Audrey Vale herself burst in wearing a large feathered hat. "Good *Gawwwwd!*" she said, projecting and spitting like a pro. "You sound like a bloody traffic jam."

"That was the largo," Dick said, "quiet as we can get." The whistle dropped from his mouth and dangled on its string. Mrs. Vale was a classy lady and implied clearly without being the least bit vulgar what Dick should do with his whistle.

She stormed out, but Dick, never intimidated, blew his whistle and got "The Thunderer" out again. At the end of it we could hear the actors stamping past our door on their way out. A formidable man whom I recognized immediately as T.H. Wholton, principal of Galt Collegiate, walked in. He was directing the play. A hush fell.

"I trust you realize you have ruined another of our rehearsals." He stared us all down until his eye came to rest on Dick's whistle. "You'll hear about this."

We never did. The Little Theatre moved out.

32
Father's Obsession

*I*n 1936, while Adolf Hitler's troops reoccupied the Rhineland and his dive bombers savaged Spain in an overt rehearsal for World War II, Canada was putting the finishing touches on its memorial to World War I, the war to end all wars. The Canadian National Vimy Memorial in France is a tribute to the 66,000 Canadians killed in the so-called Great War. Its twin spires, symbolizing Canada's two founding races, tower 226 feet above a concrete plinth that covers 40,000 square feet and is inscribed with the names of the 11,285 Canadian soldiers killed in France who have no known graves. Walter Allward, the memorial's designer, specified that it be constructed of Adriatic marble so that in his words, "It would stand for all time," to remind the world of the men who had died to make war obsolete.

Hitler, who intended to dynamite the monument when he visited the site after the fall of France in 1940, was so impressed by its solemn beauty that he changed his mind and let it stand. My father was even more impressed than Hitler by the memorial. He had stormed the ridge with the Canadian Corps in 1917.

Pierre Berton, in his epic book *Vimy*, recounts an incident my father could never forget:

> Private Green of New Hamburg struggled upwards with his battalion. Suddenly a dud shell whizzed past, barely missing him. It sliced off the head off a machine gunner and took the leg off a corporal. The severed head flew through the air like a football, struck another man and nearly felled him. And the headless corpse, blood spurting from the severed arteries, actually took two steps forward before toppling with his machine gun into the muck.

Understandably Pop became obsessed with Vimy Ridge and then with the memorial. He began to carve models of it. "Don't bother your father," my mother would tell my sister, Shirley, and me. "He's carving Vimy again." His first wooden model, painted white, towered eighteen inches and stood in the show window of Himes Brothers Smoke Shop for a week every November guarded by my toy lead models of the Gordon Highlanders.

The onset of World War II inspired Pop to start carving Vimy Mark II. He sculpted it lovingly out of the choicest walnut, and because of the beautiful wood grain, he decided not to paint it white like the original. The real memorial took eleven years to complete. Pop spent fourteen on his. He abandoned it for months, depending on the war news, but fired up by Allied victories and annual Vimy banquets he finally finished it in 1952.

Mark II, landscaped on a foot-high promontory of plywood covered with green billiard table cloth, was four times the size of Mark I and took over one end of our living room. It perched on a desk itself filled with war memorabilia and the ledgers and petty cash of the 111th Battalion. Pop was no sculptor, and the twenty symbolic figures, the mourning mother and angels scaling the towers, had faces that later reminded me of those found on Cabbage Patch dolls. My mother thought the angels' breasts were too big. "Angels don't have breasts that big," she would say.

"Mine do," Pop would counter.

Every November 11, Pop planted another poppy in the billiard cloth. His battalion beret hung on one of the towers, and our cats, Mushi and Bongo, slept between them. My mother felt with all due respect that the model should be at the Legion Hall with my father, but the Legion deferred accepting it until after Pop was gone and we sold the house in 1989.

As you might imagine, my father had always wanted to see the real Vimy Memorial and vowed to do so before he died. He was eighty-one when he finally made the pilgrimage to France in 1979. My mother, who had commitments with the Senior Citizens' Harmonica Band, didn't go with him. Pop returned reborn, loaded with Super 8 movies of flower beds blurring by his train window and clouds enveloping his plane over the English Channel. But there were no pictures of the Vimy Memorial.

My mother knew him well enough to ask him point-blank, "You did get there, didn't you?"

"Of course, quite close, in fact."

"How close?"

"To a town within twenty-five miles."

"Why didn't you go all the way?"

"I couldn't read directions in French and I was afraid I would miss my train back."

"So you didn't get there!" She rolled her eyes. "After all that you didn't get to see what you went there for."

"I got there in 1917 when it counted," Pop said, and that settled it.

33
The Air Raid Patrol

*I*n 1941 the German blitzkrieg was rolling our ill-equipped and pathetically led armies down to the shore of Dunkirk and we were scared. We saw the enemy behind every tree. Guards were posted on the Welland Canal, at every hydroelectric plant and all strategic bridges, and on the Hamilton Incline Railway. And we interned our friendliest neighbours if they were German or Italian immigrants.

Schoolchildren took classes in aircraft recognition, even though enemy bombers with the longest range would fall into the Atlantic long before they reached Newfoundland. There was talk of handing out gas masks. My uncle, Bill Spring, began practice route-marches out Cheese Factory Road all by himself so as to be physically fit when the recruiting office found his number (he wound up as a cook in the air force).

Veterans of World War I too old for another fling at the Boche couldn't sit idly by. They formed the Air Raid Patrol, ARP. I believe they were inspired by a news photo of a British clergyman, Dr. Jocelyn Henry Temple Perkins, seventy years old, standing at attention in front of his church, steel helmet on his head, a bucket of sand in one hand and a bucket of water with stirrup pump attached in the other. "I'm ready for them," he was quoted as saying.

Soon after that my father returned from the Legion Hall with two pails, a stirrup pump, and a steel helmet, courtesy of the Department of National Defence, which had also been inspired by the Reverend Perkins. My mother cautioned my sister and me not to laugh. The stirrup pump, which resembled a bicycle pump, clamped down the side of the bucket and squirted, as Pop demonstrated, a stream of water about as strong as you could do yourself if you drank a quart of water and waited half an hour. "Don't laugh," he said. "You don't need a great torrent to douse falling embers. The bucket of sand is for magnesium incendiary bombs. You can't extinguish magnesium with water."

As the Battle of Britain intensified and the newspapers filled up with the heroics of the British Home Guard dousing fires with stirrup pumps and sand, the local ARP itched for action. After the devastating bombing of Coventry, England, on November 14, the ARP decided to go into action even if it had to bomb itself. And that was what it did in an exercise on the east side of Galt. The enemy always bombed the east side of cities where the poor lived. The area to be devastated was bounded by Lowrey Avenue, where we lived, Pollock Avenue to the north, and an undisclosed number of streets south to the East Street dump.

For strategic reasons the raid was scheduled for a Tuesday evening, garbage night in our sector. The Luftwaffe, commanded by Reich Marshal Erskine Jardine, would take off in cars from the Legion Hall and set fires at random in the doomed area. It was the ARP's job to dash in and put them out. Incendiary fires to be smothered with sand were marked by little red flags. Yellow flags denoted fires to be squirted with water. My mother gave me permission to go out with kids on the block and watch the exercise as long as I kept out of the way and didn't laugh.

The first incendiary on our block hit the garbage in front of Gammon's Grocery Store at the corner of Pollock and Lincoln. Within seconds Ivan McQueen, who had been hiding behind a tree, was trowelling sand on it from one of his buckets. Good thing it was an incendiary bomb, because he spilled his bucket of water.

"Why are you laughing?" he hollered at us. "In a real air raid you would be at home in your basement."

Up and down the street ARP wardens shouted at kids until they were blue in the face. Wave after wave of Luftwaffe cars zoomed by, igniting garbage with squirts of kerosene and planting little red and yellow flags. There was confusion. "Not water on that one, stupid. It's a red flag!"

But soon a conflagration began that the ARP hadn't counted on. The autumn leaves, endless mounds of fluffy tinder-dry leaves in the gutters block after block, caught fire and, fanned by a strong north wind, were soon blazing like the London dockyards. Women and children with brooms and garden hoses rushed in to fight the infernos. Even the

Luftwaffe had to stop and lend a hand. It took the fire department to control the blaze on East Street.

When the fires were finally brought under control, the ARP, exhausted, reeking of smoke, and thirsty, retired to the war room of the Legion Hall to assess the exercise. The boys must have concluded the mock air raid was a success, because they never bothered to hold another one.

The affair certainly had lasting benefits. Pop used his stockpile of incendiary bomb sand to plant geranium slippings in his greenhouse. And the stirrup pump was just the thing for watering seedlings on the top shelves. My mother planted African violets in the steel helmet and set it in a kitchen window.

My sister, Shirley, and I kept our laughs to ourselves, but Mom wouldn't let Pop forget. "The whole town could burn down," she said. "But you'd save the Legion Hall. It would be the last building left standing."

The East Street dump burned for days.

34

Victory

The war in Europe, as fewer and fewer of us remember, ended May 8, 1945. I was in high school that morning. We were expecting the armistice but didn't know the exact moment until the factory whistles began to toot. The major factories in Galt used them to signal the start of the workday and the beginning and end of lunch. Each factory had a whistle of a distinct pitch, and we got to know where the toots came from. Gardiner's Woodworking plant had a deep-throated whistle that sounded like that of an ocean liner. All the whistles were steam. At 10:00 a.m. they all let go like a giant calliope.

I remember Mary Burrows running across the art room to fling up the window and let the sound in. Soon the church bells joined the whistles, and we all began to clap and shout inanities. Rules and regulations suspended themselves as we abandoned our desks, ran through the halls, streamed out the doors, and hurtled down Water Street Hill to Main Street.

I was on call with the Kiwanis Boys' Band. Our conductor, Dick Ellis, had told us at our last practice that as soon as the war ended we were to get to the band room in the old Gore Building, unlimber our instruments, and get set for a parade. I got there just as Dick was unlocking the door.

So far the celebration was limited mainly to drivers honking their horns and pedestrians waving back, but by the time I had harnessed my snare drum and lugged it down to the street, men and women, total strangers, were embracing shamelessly right under the traffic lights. Only the opposite sexes embraced openly in those days. Joe Burchill, fresh out of the army band but a Boys' Band alumnus, appeared with his trumpet, and I followed him into a ladies' dress shop. He blew a few bugle calls, I thumped on my drum, and the ladies got quite excited and began to dance the way my Auntie Bea did on Christmas Eve. There were whiffs of alcohol in the air. A dozen ladies in the shop all wanted to kiss us, a disconcerting experience when you were sober, fifteen, and had a snare drum strapped in front of you. A voluptuous lady, perhaps thirty years old and bursting with patriotism out of her tight black dress, threw her arms around me and said, "Hi, sonny, I'm Alice. Want to have some fun?" She had big brown eyes that looked like loosely sewn-on buttons.

"Sure," I said. "Just wait'll I get this damn snare drum unhooked." But I was drawn up sharp by a shrill whistle at the door. It was Dick Ellis, our bandmaster, covered in lipstick. He was calling for a parade.

So I had to follow Joe Burchill back outside. Half a dozen bandsmen appeared, but though Dick blew his whistle until his eyes crossed, they abandoned him to follow Joe back into the dress shop. Before I could turn to follow, Don McFadyen grabbed my shoulder and hollered that I was needed to play drums on a truck. Willis Toles had been hired to put a jazz band on a truck and play all around downtown ... for money!

A red stake truck, blowing its horn, pushed towards us through the crowd. Toles was already aboard, blasting back at the car horns on his trombone and shouting to the drivers that they were either sharp or flat.

Joe Burchill, covered with lipstick, fled the dress shop and climbed aboard. I didn't need my snare drum because an old set of drums had come with the truck.

McFadyen had gotten a bass fiddle from somewhere, and we headed off to pick up a piano out of a house near the old Galt Hospital on St. Andrews Street. Half a dozen boisterous men heaved it aboard. As the truck careened down St. Andrews Street Hill, the piano rolled out of control and threatened to crush us. Fortunately, two casters broke off and the piano fell onto its back. We pushed it upright again when the truck stopped at Main and Water. Harry "Stompy" Jones climbed aboard and started to play the piano standing up. He was covered in lipstick. Then a saxophone player, Don Kunkle, I believe, also covered in lipstick, joined us, and we really got fired up as we blasted our way through the mob to the market square.

Glenna Phaneuf, the vivacious and flamboyant ticket booth girl from the Capitol Theatre, was thrust aboard by hands in the street and announced she was about to sing. She had just applied fresh lipstick. Glenna sang "Melancholy Baby" without a microphone, and the crowd, which couldn't possibly hear her over the general din, went crazy. She threw kisses to everybody and danced with abandon to the "Sheik of Araby." She might have been Betty Hutton.

The old memory fades a bit at this point. I recall seeing the truck later that night abandoned in front of Joan's Lunch on Main Street. It had a flat tire, and someone said the driver was in jail. He had stolen the truck. And, of course, we never got paid and never cared.

The city survived the celebration with little more damage than lipstick stains. I never made it back to the ladies' dress shop. But if you're still out there, Alice, and still want to have some fun, just let me know which nursing home you're in and I'll drop by to see you with a box of Reid's mixed nuts.

35

How Roger Ruined the War

By the time Japan surrendered on August 14, 1945, we were all partied out and the occasion wasn't nearly as exciting as VE day. Anyway, we were just returning to school, and it seemed silly when the whistles and church bells let loose once more to run out the door and across the campus in search of Alice again. I can't recall any great celebration in Galt. There was a big one in the United States, of course. And in the Far East.

Roger Johnson was in Singapore that day, and his account of the victory festivities there is memorable. He told me about it years later after he moved to Preston with his wife, Mary Ellen, and established himself as a travel agent.

Lord Louis Mountbatten ran the show in Singapore and ordered up a great victory parade to pass by a reviewing stand on which he would take the salute. Roger was in the Royal Air Force, not a large military presence in that area of combat, and marched in the parade behind a thin little brass band. The Royal Navy was the big power there, and its members marched behind a formidable band as loud as the broadside of a battleship. This posed a problem when the parade followed a turning circle around a park on one side of which stood the reviewing stand. There the navy band, leading the parade, blasted past the reviewing stand with such vigour that the RAF marchers on the opposite side lost touch with their own little band.

"The RAF band," Roger said, "playing 'The Thin Red Line' was completely overpowered when the navy band struck up 'The Thunderer.' Without a thought, as soon as I lost the sound of my own band, I fell into step with the big band across the turning circle. All it took was a little hop."

Then Roger heard the man behind take a little hop and the next man beside him. He had to admit he was first. Soon the whole platoon was taking little hops to get into step with the navy. However, as they rounded the circle and headed for the reviewing stand, they regained the sound of their own band and tried to hop back into step with it. By the time they passed under the salute of Lord Mountbatten, Roger said, everyone was skipping and hopping. Lord Mountbatten, ramrod straight in his shimmering white uniform, seemed oblivious to the pandemonium passing under his nose, though his eyes bugged out and his medals trembled in the sunlight.

Back at the airfield Roger's commanding officer had some sort of seizure and began to shout. "I've been in charge of some prize fatheads," he hollered, "but you guys are the biggest shower of shit I've ever seen!" He continued in this vein for some time while the platoon stood rigidly at attention. He enumerated all the hellish campaigns he had survived through the long war: Burma, Borneo, New Guinea, where he had been wounded, and Buno-Gona, all leading excruciatingly to this day and the glorious victory parade.

"And what happens?" the commanding officer barked. "My platoon makes me look like an ass right in front of my commander-in-chief, Lord Mountbatten." Then, wiping the froth off his mouth with the back of his hand, he said in the same tone he might have used when he was wounded. "Johnson." Twice he said it. "Johnson, I'm told you were the first to break step."

"That's quite possible," Roger said.

"Well, you've ruined the war for me, Johnson, the whole fucking war. How do you like that?"

Roger couldn't remember what he said. But afterwards he thought, *What a silly row. All I did was get out of step. Mountbatten organized Dieppe.*

36
More About Roger

I had heard about Roger Johnson for years before I met him. People kept telling me, "You've got to meet Roger. He's Irish and so is his wife, Mary Ellen. You'll love them. They're both crazy. He's a fine artist who paints sailing ships and sells them out of Tall Ships Studio in Toronto."

And someone would say, "Here's a Roger Johnson story," and it would be Irish and hilarious.

Roger gathered many loyal friends who flocked to his travel agency. The trouble was that few of them could afford to travel anywhere. "Not to worry," Roger would tell them. "Just between you and me travel is a degenerate waste of time, particularly if you fancy going to Florida. But if you insist and can't afford the limo, I'll drive you to the airport myself." And that he did in a car whose door on the driver side was secured with a rope. He spent his own holidays with his family in a cottage loaned to him by friends in Port Dover.

In order to concentrate on painting sailing ships, Roger always wanted to retire, and he even sold his agency once but wound up working harder than ever for the new owner. "I have three brilliant children in school who eat and eat," he would say. "I'm afraid I'm going to retire feet first." Which he ultimately did.

Mary Ellen, Roger's wife, was his total match. She called him "the block character." When she spelled him at the agency, she would say, "Okay, I'm covering for you, now go and play."

"Go *and play!*" he would roar. "Did you hear what she said?"

Roger loved to roar. He coached a girls' soccer team and roared with such enthusiasm that the girls, who invariably lost, sometimes thought they had won. And the winning team, hearing the cheering from the other end of the field after a game, must have wondered who had really lost.

So I was well acquainted with Roger by the time we finally met over the phone. "Roger Johnson here," he said, "a fellow artist in need." And he asked me if I could help him out of a bit of a mess. His one-man show of sailing ships was to open in three days at the Preston Library gallery, and he was short of paintings and wondered if I would like to add a few of my own and make it a two-man show.

I was thrilled to share a show with Roger and met him at the gallery within the hour. He looked as he sounded on the phone. Very Irish. He was stocky and had a thick shock of grizzled hair and moved briskly while sweeping his arms about with authority. The size of the tiny gallery astounded him, and he fussed aloud to himself about how on earth he could fill it.

"Take any wall you want," he said.

"But I brought only three paintings," I said.

"Then fetch some more, all you want, in fact. You can have equal space."

"Great," I said.

"Actually," he said, forming a frame with his hands and squinting through it, "you can take three of the walls."

"There are only four," I said.

"Right on, but the more I look at the space the more I know I can only do justice to one."

"How many paintings do you have?" I asked.

He started ticking them off on his fingers and got up to five. Then he backed down to three.

I thought he was joking. "Three?" I said.

"Three." He wasn't joking. "The trouble is," he added, "they're not in frames."

"Then you can't hang them."

"Right."

"Can you get them framed in three days?"

"No."

"Then you have no pictures for the show."

"That's right. Not a single blarsted one."

And that was how I got my first one-man show at the Preston Library.

As he prophesied, before he could retire, he died of a heart attack. Suddenly, like an earthquake. Devastating to all who knew him. I'm still not sure whether it was ten years ago or the day before yesterday. I still here him hollering when I pass a soccer field. "We got 'em where we want 'em, girls. Press on!"

37

Lucky Eddy Martin

Bing McCauley was a great friend of Lucky Eddy Martin, so called because of the disasters that befell him everywhere. I might mention that this Eddy Martin shouldn't be confused with Eddy Martin, the bass fiddle player who lived in Preston. Lucky Eddie Martin played piano, but just as a hobby and only so long as he had enough fingers left to do it.

Lucky Eddy worked with Bing McCauley's dad, Bob McCauley, at Galt Metal Industries back in the 1940s but should never have worked with metal because he kept losing fingers in the machines. Bing said that whenever he waved to Eddy across the street he seemed to have fewer fingers to wave back with. No matter how many fingers were missing, though, Eddy enthusiastically played the piano, substituting missing fingers with ones held in reserve like troops at the front.

Eddy was an affable man and easy company, and Bing's dad often took him home for dinner. Mrs. McCauley said she was nervous all the time he was there for fear his cigarette might set fire to the house. Eddy boarded with Alex "Sandy" Ford on Beverly Street in Galt. Daughter Helen Ford, then a teenager, told how one day her brothers came home to find the house full of smoke. It was, of course, Eddy asleep on a smouldering mattress. They had to push the mattress out the window and drag Eddy off to the hospital, suffering from smoke inhalation. He boarded with the Fords for twelve years, and it was a marvel that any of them survived. Helen said they all loved him.

Because Eddy had wrecked so many cars, he was no longer allowed to drive and had to walk to work. But cars wouldn't leave him in peace. He was run over one day at the intersection of Main and Ainslie. Not long after he got out of the hospital and was hobbling on crutches past the old Imperial Bank at Main and Water, a painter doing the eaves high above dropped a gallon of paint on his shoulder. Back to the hospital Eddy went with a broken collarbone, numerous cuts and bruises, and a suit he had just bought drenched with green paint. Not a cheap suit, either, because Eddy was a dapper dresser.

When Eddy recovered from that disaster, Bob McCauley treated him to a night out at a hockey game in the Galt Arena. The only puck to fly into the crowd hit Eddy on the ear, and back to the hospital he went again. It got so that every time an ambulance went by people would say "Poor Eddy."

Some people complain a lot about their misfortunes, but never Eddy. He might have had to smile through bandages and wave greetings with a cast on his arm, but he was always cheerful, optimistic even, and an inspiration to everyone. Friends hesitated to visit him, though, for fear of hearing him fall down the stairs on his way to answer the door. And some people kept their distance for fear some of his luck might hurtle their way. Bob McCauley told of visiting a friend in the hospital who was gravely ill. He beckoned Bob to the bedside to whisper a word, possibly his last. "Bob," he gasped, "promise me you won't bring Lucky Eddy up to visit." Bob didn't and the man survived.

Lucky Eddy died in a car accident while heading for a holiday near Kincardine in 1977. Cars were out to get him. Everything was out to get him.

38

More Lore from Bing

*B*ing McCauley followed in his father's and Lucky Eddy Martin's footsteps and landed a job at Galt Metal Industries in the 1950s. The firm made mufflers for Ford in Windsor. One day Bing's boss called him into his office and said Ford was sending up a quality-control inspector to check out the plant. He reasoned that if he and Bing gave the rep a good time at some of the local high spots, increased orders for mufflers would follow.

The inspector's name was Jim Nolan. After his whirlwind tour of the plant, the three went to lunch at the Plainsman Restaurant (noted for its fine buffet) north of Dundas. It was also one of the few restaurants then licensed to serve beer. Bing said they had a lot of laughs and forgot all about mufflers. From there they drove to the Paris Golf Club for nine leisurely holes. "It was sweltering hot," Bing said, "but fortunately the golf club had an adequate supply of cold beer."

By the time they got back to Galt, dehydration had struck again and Bing suggested they top up at the Overland Hotel. Nolan was delighted with the Overland's frontier atmosphere and was putting his stamp of approval on everything. Soon after they sat down and adjusted their eyes to the dim light they watched a fight break out between a customer who was drunk and a waiter who refused to serve him. The Overland was then owned by Mayor Arthur White, who was trying to get a little class into the place. The waiter couldn't wrestle the drunk alone, and Arthur, who didn't believe in delegating the dirty work, waded in to help. The three tussled desperately around the tables until they slipped on the sawdust and fell in a heap.

Bing said to Nolan, "See that big guy in the white shirt rolling in the sawdust, the one on top now putting on the arm lock? He's the mayor of Galt."

Nolan's jaw dropped. "Bull!" he said. "Bull!"

"He is," Bing insisted. "That's Arthur White, our mayor."

"Bull!"

Nolan continued to enjoy his quality-control trips to Galt. Several years later while dining out with Bing and his boss at another hotel he said, "That guy we saw wrestling in the sawdust in that dump, the one you told me was mayor of Galt ... is he still the mayor?"

"Not anymore," Bing said. "Now Arthur is our Member of Parliament."

"Bull!" Nolan said. "Bull!"

After Arthur became a Member of Parliament, he answered his phone saying, "This is Arthur White, MP and BA."

39

Our Nutty Dentists

Galt certainly had its share of eccentric dentists. When I wanted a day off school and needed a note from my parents, I went to the dentist. Dr. Fennel would write me a note.

"What would you like to be off with this time?" he would ask. "Not the flu again. We've milked that. How about pink eye?"

"How about an abscessed tooth?" I would suggest.

"I can't write notes involving teeth. That's malpractice. Let's make it pink eye. And that's your quota for the month. Tell Don MacFadyen he's had his quota, too. I wrote him a note for pink eye this morning."

Dr. Fennel wrote notes for lots of kids. He said if they had enough intelligence to play hooky they might turn into dentists someday. But Dr. Fennel was really a conservative eccentric. Just a block up Main Street, Dr. Lorne Winter, one of the most accomplished dentists around, extracted teeth free of charge and without freezing in the Iroquois Hotel beer parlour. He carried his dental tools everywhere in a little black bag.

The grand champion eccentric had to be Dr. Harold Mason, the metaphysical hypno-dentist who kept the Royal College of Dentists' Disciplinary Committee grinding its teeth for thirty years. He was a phenomenal hypnotist. Teeth came out and fillings went in without pain or chemical anesthesia. Harvey McClellan from the *Galt Reporter* composing room had nine teeth out one morning and went right back to work.

"No pain," Dr. Mason would say in a singsong voice, "no pain at all, and after I count down to one from ten there will be no pain for three days." He always threw in the three extra painless days. The fourth day, however, was always hell. He did this to demonstrate his control and put down the doubters.

Sometimes when the dental work was finished, rather than waste a good trance, Dr. Mason led patients through startling extrasensory experiences. He told me one day while I was awaiting the countdown for a wisdom tooth extraction that he had just that morning projected a lady patient to the surface of the moon and had her describe graphically the craters there.

Friday was psychosomatic night at the Mason clinic. No teeth to fix, just nasty habits like smoking, compulsive eating, and window peeping.

Patients came from Hamilton, London, and all around, and Dr. Mason would put them into deep trances and shout at their subconscious. "No more raisin pie! No more! And no more sticky-icky Coke!" he would command. His authority even to the onlooker was riveting.

Dr. Mason didn't mind if you dropped in to watch, and he was easy on confidentiality. "This teenage girl in the dental chair," he would say, "she can't hear us." And he would croon in her ear, "Can't hear, Carol, can't hear at all. She wants to stop drinking Coke so she won't get fat like her mother. But the real reason she's here is that her parents want me to stop her from running around with the boys and getting drunk. Can't hear, Carol, can't hear. I treat both her parents for migraines. That's her mother in the flowered dress on the couch over there. The bald guy on the other couch is her father. He's principal of Lakeview Collegiate. They drive up from Fisherville every Friday night. The girl is hopeless. Her mother runs around and her father doesn't know. Can't hear, can't hear. I'm treating him for impotence."

The hypno-dentist treated people for everything, and not just by shouting at their subconscious. Some of his lady patients revealed in subsequent court appearances that he had treated their arthritis and bowel irregularities with animal magnetism. That was what Dr. Mason called it when he trolled his hands over their afflicted organs so as to draw out the pain. The police were always trying to trap him.

"I spotted that policewoman in the low-cut dress as soon as she waltzed into my office," he told the court in his last appearance. "Fortunately, I am seventy-two and was able to resist." He always maintained that you couldn't explain science to the police.

Dr. Mason didn't match the popular conception of a great hypnotist: dashing, slim, goateed, large blazing eyes, decked out in a top hat and a cape. He was more like a potbellied Pooh bear, gimlet-eyed, moon-faced, and bald. And while you mused over this in his dental chair until you assumed he couldn't hypnotize anyone, he would hypnotize you. He extracted an infected wisdom tooth from my mouth without pain even while I tried in vain to signal I wasn't hypnotized.

He was mystified by his own powers, his ability to cure (temporarily, anyway) smoking, snoring, and impotence. "Impotence," he said, his mind leaping with abandon, "was Hitler's big hang-up." And he implied that if he had had a clinic in Berlin in the 1930s there would have been no World War II.

Dentistry was too small a pond for a frog of Dr. Mason's stature, so he took to demonstrating his powers on the world stage, starting with the service club circuit.

In 1958 he was the entertainment one night for a service club in Brantford. Bridey Murphy, who retrogressed into former lives, was all the rage then, and Dr. Mason put his entranced subject, a Galt man named Jim, through all the gears: retrogression, transmigration, astral projection and, for an encore, clairvoyance. With his subject in the clairvoyant state, Dr. Mason invited members of the audience to pose questions on any matter. Someone asked, "What happened to Mabel Crumbach?

Mabel Crumbach was a woman who had disappeared while travelling from Toronto to Hamilton some years before and was still the object of a police search.

In his trance Jim saw her get into a car with Michigan licence plates and follow a circuitous route through Brantford. He drew a map, noting streets and service stations. The car, he said, then headed south out of Brantford on a country road and stopped by a field where the woman was then buried close to some cedar trees. He gave the numbers on the Michigan licence plate. Needless to say this caused a stir. After a sleepless night, one of the service club members called the police. The police got Dr. Mason to put Jim back into the trance of the night before and repeat the question about Mabel Crumbach, then set off for Brantford in a police cruiser.

"Turn right here, now turn left," Jim said, repeating the Michigan licence number. At last on a side road south of Brantford Jim said, "Stop!" and pointed to a pasture spotted with cedar trees. "She's buried there." The police promptly roped off the field and started digging. Jim hadn't pointed to any particular spot, just the whole field.

The story hit the front pages of most newspapers in Southern Ontario. There were photos of policemen, unaccustomed to this sort of exertion, sweating and swearing. We all held our breath. The Royal College of Dentists' Disciplinary Committee, muscles bunching, didn't know whether to prepare a special citation for Dr. Mason or heat up the tar and feathers.

After several days of trenching the field and finding no body, the Ontario Provincial Police officer in charge mopped his brow and confronted Dr. Mason. "The dig is over. It's a flop."

"Don't give up so easily," Dr. Mason said. "Jim is sometimes a little off. Why not start on the field across the road?"

The officer wasn't easily hypnotized. Nor was the Michigan State Police, which called to say the licence number offered up in Jim's trance didn't exist. It was over. The Royal College of Dentists' Disciplinary Committee huffed itself up. "Just as we thought," it said among other things. Then it heaved a great sigh of relief. So did everybody else.

40

Green Nile Compost

*I*n the 1950s a little man on Glenmorris Street in Galt claimed to have developed a super soil compost that would save world agriculture. His card said he was Stanley J. Hartman, Doctor of Metaphysics, STD, PhD, DSC, Director of the Canadian Metaphysical and Organic Research Institute, with degrees from Queen's, McGill, and Heidelberg universities.

"If you don't believe me," he would say, "ask me."

He was also the regional director of the Rosicrucian Society.

Dr. Hartman lived on Glenmorris Street with Mr. and Mrs. Rollins, who gave him shelter from his detractors. They also helped him process his super compost in their backyard and built him a laboratory on the side of their garage. In his laboratory he produced a key ingredient that made his compost super, but the gist of it came from the Kitchener sewage treatment plant in a yellow Austin dump truck. The sewage was garnished with weeds from ditches along the way and some special leaves that blew into the Rollinses' yard from trees around the West Side Gospel Chapel next door.

After this roughage was fed through a shredding machine, Dr. Hartman would emerge from his laboratory with a vial of "Green Nile" concentrate, sprinkle it on the pile, make some passes with his hands, and stand back to await the "aura." The day I was there everyone present saw the aura — a rainbow halo over the pile. At Dr. Hartman's insistence I began to see it myself.

He hoped to stockpile his compost on a farm to be bought through the sale of a Stradivarius violin that had fortuitously turned up in Mrs. Rollins's hands. She showed the violin on Kitchener television, but there were no takers. Dr. Hartman was appalled. The world's soil, he said, was turning into Plasticine and civilization would soon cry out for his compost. To hasten research and buy the farm, his associates, seven in all, sold Green Nile Compost door to door at $1 a bag.

My father was also an authority on soil. He had sold from his little lean-to greenhouse on Lowrey Avenue the best tomato plants in Galt for forty years, and without a vendor's licence. When I told him about Dr. Hartman's super compost, he howled with laughter. When I told him how they were selling it door to door at $1 a bag, he stopped.

"What did you say they called it?" he asked.

"Green Nile."

"Does it look this?" he said, and held up a five-pound bag. A second bag leaned against his chair.

"Yes."

"Damn! That must have been them at the door this afternoon."

41

Dr. Hartman Scuttles History

Dr. Stanley J. Hartman told me that as director of the Canadian Metaphysical and Organic Research Institute his greatest fear was the possibility of his organization becoming infested with screwballs like those in the government. It was essential, he said, to keep his staff and membership level-headed for the day they would have to negotiate with extraterrestrials.

That day beckoned on August 3, 1957, when a landing was reported in a field just north of the Alps Road at the rear of our future fairgrounds.

A shy and unpretentious boy, Jack Stephenson, fourteen, came to the *Galt Reporter* office the next afternoon and related a most improbable story to senior reporter Roy Francis. He had told the story to his mother who believed him and thought it shouldn't be kept secret. They first figured he should tell the police, but considered that the *Reporter* would be more sympathetic.

Young Stephenson had been walking his dog in a field where hydroelectric high-tension wires passed between three small ponds. A flash in the sky caught his eye, and he looked up to see what he described as a saucer-shaped craft descend and make a soft landing close to one of the ponds. Stephenson watched from behind a tree with his madly barking dog while the craft, humming to itself, rested for forty-five minutes. Nothing spectacular happened — no little green men or anything — until the craft slowly rose and, silently accelerating, disappeared straight overhead.

Francis accompanied Stephenson back to the field. Within the hour Francis returned as excited as I have ever seen a man. He ran over to my desk. "The marks are there," he said, eyes bugging out. "You've got to see them." After he dashed off an alarming and hysterical story for the next day's paper, he rushed back to the field and took me with him.

There was certainly lots of evidence. Three foot-long claw-shaped marks pressed eight inches into the drought-hardened ground in a nine-foot triangle at the centre of which a wide circle of soil was burnt black to the depth of an inch or more. Nearby bales of hay were smashed and scattered over a wide area. Within thirty feet of the burnt circle a small arc of poplar trees, beside a pond, were snapped off precisely three feet above the ground, their frayed stumps making it clear they hadn't been chopped. Several of them were more than four inches thick. We decided the evidence wouldn't support a hoax.

Roy Francis's sensational story in the next day's *Reporter* featured photos he took of the marks, including an excellent close-up of one of the "claw" marks and a drawing of the alleged spacecraft based on Stephenson's description.

The front-page story went over Canadian Press and caused quite a flap everywhere. Sleuths from the Canadian and U.S. military flew in to check out the field. They included two Royal Canadian Air Force special investigators and Commander Donald Keyhoe of the U.S. Navy. UFOs were then taken seriously. The unprecedented physical evidence on the ground offered a rare opportunity for interpretation and could have altered the course of civilization. But the investigators were too late.

At dawn, the day after the *Reporter* story, Dr. Hartman and a special detail from his Metaphysical Institute descended on the landing site, dug up all the evidence, and hustled it in burlap bags back to the laboratory on Glenmorris Street. Later, crowds of sightseers trampled everything Dr. Hartman missed.

Military authorities were appropriately distressed and spoke with threatening tones about a "local man trying to take over the investigation." They were, in fact, in a frothing rage. Dr. Hartman himself told me about the visit he had from two RCAF officers at his laboratory.

"I had just carefully loaded all the diggings into glass jars and wrapped them in lead foil to control the radiation when there was this hammering on the door. Two men in blue uniforms stormed in. One of them asked me if I was the Dr. Hartman who had without authority dug up the landing site. I told them they should be thankful I rescued the evidence before somebody ruined it and that after I studied it I would release a report that they could have if they applied in writing. Well, talk about rude! They were what you might call ignorant. Swore a lot. One of them even lit up a cigarette. Now you never light a cigarette in a laboratory, especially right under the picture of Jesus. I told them to get the hell out, and they left in a hurry. I stand up to the military."

Dr. Hartman squinted through the thumbprints on his thick spectacles and broke into a maniacal laugh. "It's a good thing I have a sense of humour," he said. "If I didn't, in this business I'd go batty."

The space visitors, as far as we know, never returned. Dr. Hartman, who was later run over by a truck in New York City, has departed and may well be with the extraterrestrials. Roy Francis, also departed now, ripped his pants on a fence while doing his story and never received a cent of compensation from the *Reporter*.

Dr. Hartman's intentions were good, but in his course of duty he obliterated what was arguably the greatest scientific epiphany in the history of the world. Pity.

The day after Roy Francis's story-of-a-lifetime the *Reporter* became preoccupied with traffic congestion at the junction of Highway 8 and Coronation Boulevard. A year after the event a psychology professor from Toronto, Martin Greenwood, researching first-hand UFO sightings for a project at Dunlap Observatory, questioned Stephenson at length, pronounced him sane, said he believed he was telling the truth, and gave him $1 for the interview.

95

42

Werstine and Herbert

My last view of the ill-fated *Cambridge Reporter*'s editorial room, half a dozen journalists quietly fussing with their computers in smoke-free cubicles complete with ashtrays heaped with potato chips, gave me flashbacks to the same room fifty years earlier — chaotic, noisy, and blue with cigarette smoke.

Staffers pecked with two fingers on ancient manual typewriters that had at least one key stuck and hollered from one desk to another news that had come in on the wrong phone. Earl Werstine, editor emeritus and author of the "Around the Town" column, alone had privacy. He laboured in a tiny office built around a pillar by the stairs leading to the composing room. Bill Herbert, managing editor, said the office was built specifically to hide Werstine's disgusting spittoon.

Werstine would burst from his office and shuffle to the city desk like an old yard engine, belching great clouds of cigar smoke and methane gas. "Where's Herbert?" he would holler.

Herbert, standing in front of him, would say, "Three guesses."

They were like Laurel and Hardy.

For years after 3:00 p.m. they left the office together to go to the Iroquois Hotel beer parlour, which they called the Main Street Bureau, the source of much of Werstine's daily column. Herbert joined Alcoholics Anonymous and sipped ginger ale at the Iroquois, but Werstine soldiered on. He said he had intended to quit drinking but changed his mind after seeing what abstinence did to Herbert. Herbert gave him a rough time.

Werstine was forgetful, and Herbert claimed the beer was giving him Korsakov's syndrome. Korsakov's syndrome is a memory deficit that afflicts long-term heavy drinkers. It was discovered, as you might guess, by a teetotalling doctor named Korsakov. Herbert said that Werstine thought Korsakov's syndrome was a Russian symphony.

"Stick Korsakov," Werstine said.

"Just be glad the doctor's name wasn't Clap," Herbert said.

One day Herbert concocted a cute story about an injured mouse that crawled to a music store and asked for mouse organs. Werstine ran it in his column. Two weeks later Herbert told him the same story, and Werstine ran it again. When Herbert pointed this out, Werstine said, "Well, you're in worse shape than me. You forgot you told me the same story twice."

Normie Knechtel, the city editor, performed amazingly well considering he had to cope with both Herbert and Werstine and had never in his life touched alcohol. He did, however, have low blood pressure, which under stress caused him to faint at his desk. When the spell came over him, he retreated to the file room (morgue, in newspaper parlance) and lay down on the reading table.

One day I went to the files and didn't notice Normie until I sat down to peruse some clippings. I hollered to Werstine, who was shuffling by, "Hey! Normie's out cold on the reading table."

"Good," Werstine said. "We were looking for him." And he hollered to Herbert, "Normie's turned up on the reading table."

"I know," Herbert said. "I helped you carry him there." And he winked at me. "Don't tell me you forgot. Your cigar's out, too."

Werstine shuffled up to me and asked, "Did you see me help Herbert carry Normie to the reading table?"

"I wasn't looking," I said.

Sucking on his lifeless cigar, Werstine said, "Herbert didn't quit drinking soon enough. He's got that damn Korsakov. What a hell of a way to run a newspaper."

Before the *Reporter* moved from its Water Street office to the new Thomson Building on Ainslie, members of the staff who indulged in performance-enhancing substances threw their empty bottles into the Grand River. In summer the bottles drifted harmlessly down to Brantford to form glass jams under the Lorne Bridge. But in winter they gathered on the ice behind the *Reporter* building. Snow, which we could count on in those days, covered the bottles up, but come a thaw and they formed a squalid fan of multi-coloured glass opposite Central United Church. When Allan Holmes, the publisher, decided to run for

97

a seat on the Galt City Council, he forbade the chucking of bottles out the back because he didn't want the electors to think his decent family newspaper was produced by a bunch of drunks.

High on the wall behind Werstine's desk was a large hole where a furnace pipe had once run. Under Holmes's new edict everyone threw their bottles into the hole. After the paper moved to Ainslie Street, renovators of the old building had to leap back from an avalanche of glass when they tore down Werstine's wall. Werstine got blamed for every bottle, of course, though few were his, but he never defended himself. He just snorted a cloud of cigar smoke.

I was the wire editor in the 1950s, and one day I found a half-empty mickey of rye jamming the float in the editorial lavatory water closet. Herbert immediately blamed Werstine and Werstine blamed Herbert. However, after much thought, Herbert decided we should leave the bottle where it was because he had reason to suspect it belonged to Allan Holmes.

Contrary to the popular image of Werstine as a hard-drinking, chain-smoking curmudgeon, an image I suspect he secretly liked, he was really quite puritanical and, when writing about his love of dogs, sentimental mush. He raised a great Victorian row when the Mill Street bus station was remodelled in the 1950s and renamed the Comfort Station. What riled Earl most was the translucent glass bricks enclosing the stairwell leading to the ladies' lavatory in the basement. One could see fuzzy silhouettes descending the stairs. "This is indecent," he thundered in his column. "You can actually see where the ladies are going!"

Werstine wrote six columns a week for years, one thousand words per column, a prodigious feat. Everything that passed through his eyes and ears turned up in his column. In a 1967 column he repeated a poem he had heard about Miss McHoul, who taught all classes at St. Mary's School on Rose Street.

> The devil flew from north to south
> With Miss Nosey in his mouth,
> But when he found she was a fool
> He dropped her off at the separate school.

In the same column he noted that the cost of Gurd's ginger ale had risen 2 cents, that a flock of evening grosbeaks was spotted on Highman Avenue, and that the Valens conservation dam was taking on water early. This and much more in one sentence mercifully free of punctuation. Herbert said he was way ahead of his time.

It was common newspaper practice to prepare obituaries of notable citizens in advance of the terminal event in case the editor misplaced his thesaurus. Herbert and Werstine delighted in writing each other's obits, and left them around the office for the other to find.

One day Herbert showed me an obituary he had written for Werstine in case I had anything to add. It went: "Earl Werstine, beloved columnist on the *Galt Reporter* for most of our life spans, died peacefully today in his office at the Iroquois Hotel beverage room surrounded by many of his confidants. He wrote a well-tolerated column in spite of his being almost totally illiterate and irresponsible. The bartender ordered a free round in his honour. One for the priest, too."

And one of Werstine's eulogies for Herbert went: "Bill Herbert, our managing editor, died today of a gas attack on the toilet nearest the proof press. He wasn't a bad editor, even though he shouted a lot, drooled, quit drinking, and couldn't stop hitching up his pants. There was nothing AA could do for him."

Herbert never let on when he found his obits and would quietly crumple them and drop them into his wastebasket. He didn't want to give Werstine any satisfaction. Werstine, on the other hand, would stomp his into the floor or deposit them ceremoniously into his spittoon.

One day Earl was in a terrible car accident at an intersection north of Roseville. One man in the car, Toots Skelly, died, and Earl wasn't expected to live. Herbert, truly dismayed, sat right down and wrote a glorious tribute to his old buddy, ranking him among some of the great newspaper columnists of all time, extolling his sincerity and sobriety, his love of gardening, his fascination with steam trains, and his concern for animal welfare and his lovely wife and grandchildren. On and on it went. King George VI didn't draw higher praise.

However, Mr. Werstine, fitted with a plate in his head, survived, and one day, unannounced, puffing cigar smoke like a yard engine, he shuffled into his office and began to peck out a column about people he had met in the hospital. Herbert, by this time, had had Werstine's obituary set in lead on a composing room galley, ready to roll at the toll of the church bell. He had forgotten about it, but a thoughtful compositor ran one off on the proof press and dropped it on Earl's desk. Obit squished in his fist, Werstine stomped up to Herbert. "This is the worst yet!" he hollered. "This is disgusting. It's sacrilegious." And he tore it into bits as small as confetti and sprinkled them all over Herbert's desk and bald head.

And that ended the obituary contest.

Earl is long gone but honoured in the Cambridge Hall of Fame.

43

The Raid Next Door

I, recall one day when the *Galt Reporter* was delayed by a police raid on a bookie next door. I was wire editor at the time, Earl Werstine was still there hitting the spittoon, and Bill Herbert was managing editor.

Right after lunch Herbert clomped up the stairs from the pressroom like a bull elephant with a mouse up his trunk. "The OPP have raided the variety next door, and Ab Hogan and Archie Waring are locked in." The variety had been a betting shop in good standing for many years, so it was a mystery why it was being raided. Hattie Musclow had already placed the day's bets for editorial and the pressroom. It was one of her jobs. Rick Crossey placed the bets for advertising, so Hogan and Waring had no business being there.

Only Ab Hogan had the right to push the button that started the press. It was a union rule. So the press sat there, muscles bunching, with its crew helplessly looking on. Herbert paced the floor, hitching up his pants, and Werstine, who had bet $5, wondered if he would get his money back.

After an hour of fretting, Herbert went next door and peered through the front door. Ab and Archie were at the rear of the store eating chocolate bars. They waved. A lady brushed by, tried the door, and knocked. A plainclothes officer unlocked the door and asked her what she wanted. She handed him a note and a $10 bill to be placed on Sportsman in the third at Woodbine. The officer invited her in and locked the door. Through the glass Herbert saw her burst into tears. Another secretary under arrest.

Finally, risking all for freedom of the press, Herbert knocked on the door. The police let him in, and he made an impassioned plea for the release of Ab and Archie. The police relented and let the two go to start their press. The shop proprietor looked at Herbert. There would, of course, have to be a news story on the raid. "Don't worry, Joe," Herbert whispered. "I'll keep it small, on page 15."

Herbert always kept his word.

44
Alfie Lee

The most colourful character at the *Galt Reporter* aside from Earl Werstine had to be Alfie Lee, the janitor. He was an elf of a man who kept the newsroom so spotlessly flooded that the staff skated about their work and visitors held on to desks for dear life. Forever in rubber boots, or Wellies as he called them in his slow Cockney, Alfie bumped like a tugboat around our desks, towing his mop bucket, squinting through his telescopic spectacles, and mumbling good cheer over our shoulders. We loved him.

I recall one day when Jimmy May, of May's Farms, an ordained preacher of the Wings of Healing Society, came in to pray for us as he often did. He said we needed it. Jimmy knelt by Claude Kewley, who certainly needed it and prayed boisterously, gripping Claude's left hand while he wrote with his right. Alfie, head bowed as in church, mopped a circle around the Reverend May, leaving a dry little island that he flooded like the return of the Red Sea as soon as the prayer was over.

Alfie was really a sixty-nine-year-old boy who had never lost his enthusiasm for anything. Most of all he loved fire trucks and, of course, fires. When he first told you of some of the great fires he had seen, you couldn't help but wonder if he had set them. But one look in his eyes told you that wasn't possible, that he simply enjoyed good fires as they chanced along. Lucky that Alfie came to board with Ted and Edith Petty on Dickson Street, because Ted was a fireman and the fire hall was directly across the road. The site where their house once sat is now Petty Place.

Airplanes were another one of Alfie's passions, and his greatest thrill ever came during a flight over Brantford when he spotted a fire on the ground below. He also loved retirement parties, especially his own held to honour his years of service with the *Reporter*. They got better year after year. And each morning after he retired Alfie returned to work as usual, Wellies and all, to thank everyone over their shoulders for the lovely parting gifts he had received. No one questioned his return. It was just good to have him back.

At his third, maybe fourth, retirement party Alfie received money for a hot air balloon ride and a loud tie that really caught his fancy. Fiery red it was. He wore it to work the next day and showed it off as he sloshed around our desks. Bill Herbert caught me grinning. "Don't laugh," he said. "Some day we will all be doing this."

45
History of Our Moral Decline — It Started in Hespeler

Our present state of moral collapse, though delightful, inspired social activist Erika Kubassek to publish her apocalyptic book *One Moment to Midnight*, foretelling the Lord's terrible judgment about to descend. This is an issue I don't debate with Mrs. Kubassek when we have tea together.

However, as I put together this book, I became increasingly disturbed by our moral decline over the past century, abetted and accelerated by regional government, and I wondered if I might be able to pinpoint when and where it all began, the moment of our exodus from the peony plot in Soper Park, so to speak.

A story recounted by Percy "Punch" Harvey leads me to believe that our downward slide was started by free beer. Mr. Harvey held every important municipal post in Hespeler for half a century and was a power in the Conservative Party. During the Great Depression, when people were broke but rarely stole, left their doors unlocked, and had no qualms about letting their children play games in the woods after dark, political corruption, at the local level, anyway, was elementary to the verge of innocence. Politicians contesting the riding of South Waterloo, embracing Galt, Preston, Hespeler, Ayr, St. Agatha, Mannheim, New Dundee, and Haysville, a vast area scarcely governable, powered their campaigns with no greater vice than rounds of free beer in the beverage rooms. No enticements of mother's allowance, free trade, or tax cuts. Just free beer.

Beer was 5 cents a glass, so a round might cost $1. The candidate glad-handed his way from table to table, followed by a waiter who would say, "Keep your hands in your pockets, boys. This round is on your Liberal candidate." It was important, Mr. Harvey said, that the candidate himself not say this. There followed an hour later the same communion with the Tory candidate.

The moral turn, I believe, came during an election in the 1930s when, for no other reason than divine intervention, the Liberals were flush with money and the Tories were broke and too poor to buy a round. So to keep democracy on the level playing field the Tory campaign manager (and Mr. Harvey strongly hinted it was he) made deals with the hotel managers to deliver free rounds of beer in the name of the Tory candidate but charge them to the Liberals. The Liberals didn't learn of this treachery until they read it here. And they lost the election to boot.

This small scam, trivial compared with the SkyDome and Pearson International Airport scandals and former Ontario premier Ernie Eves's "Magna" budget, nevertheless was the same in principle and arguably the start of political corruption in Ontario. Thereafter, it seems, moral integrity everywhere began to crumble.

For instance, soon after that 1930s election, the chief of police of Hespeler, Tom Wilson, caught a party of men drinking beer from a case on the grass embankment behind the Queen's Hotel. This cost less than drinking beer in the hotel but was illegal. The chief dutifully confiscated the beer but laid no charges. They were his friends: Mike Gorman, Herman Knock (Bert Brown's father-in-law), and a few others whose names are withheld pending notification of next of kin.

One week later the chief was surprised to catch the same men drinking beer on the same spot. Again, with apologies, he confiscated their beer without charges being laid.

Not one for pouring confiscated beer down the drain, the chief served it up at a Hespeler meeting of local police chiefs, including Robert Carson of Galt, convened to discuss the growing problem of bootlegging in their jurisdictions. Unknown to Chief Wilson, the boys behind the Queen's had peed in the second batch of beer and then hammered the tops of the bottles back on. Wilson never bothered them again.

Subsequently, bootlegging thrived, bookies proliferated, churches sponsored full-frontal bingos, and gambling dens operated with impunity — one in the basement of Johnson's Grocery Store right across from the Galt police station in City Hall on Dickson Street. My uncle, Bill Spring, ran a craps table there.

Sins of the flesh flourished behind closed doors as always (the OPP raid on the Highway Garage brothel hit the front page of *Flash Weekly*), but public nudity didn't flash its flanks until the Ballet African came to the Capitol Theatre in 1957.

46

The Ballet African

The Ballet African was a troupe of bare-breasted dancers driven by drummers in fur jocks hammering on logs. First it was just a rumour. It had taken Montreal and Toronto by storm … but here! At our Capitol Theatre! The Capitol was *How Green Was My Valley* and *Gulliver's Travels*. Children went to matinees unescorted. The closest the Capitol had come to sex and sadism was *The Ten Commandments* starring Charlton Heston. Clark Gable had said "damn" in *Gone with the Wind*, but that was long forgiven.

It was a decent place. Bert Peters in a maroon-and-navy uniform complete with cap and epaulettes took your ticket in the lobby and held the lineup to sell you piano sheet music of his own compositions such as "Waka Waka Kau," a Hawaiian medley, and "Over the Hill to Grandma," a lovely waltz. He would autograph them, too. No bare breasts at the Capitol.

The first newspaper ads and posters on hydro poles drew gasps. The breasts were there all right, silhouetted, but the nipples showed. "From Darkest Africa," the promotion read, "from the headwaters of the Upper Limpopo." Savage art. Actually, the whole troupe was from New Jersey and needed clearance from the Kitchener branch of the musicians' union.

Evangelists, ignited, tore down the posters and stamped on them. A Pentecostal preacher called for a human chain to bar patrons from attending the theatre. Letters to the editor prophesied plagues of locusts. Such was the adverse publicity that the Friday and Saturday evening shows were sold out in advance and a Saturday matinee was ordered to handle the overflow.

I went with a friend, Len Iseler, a highly respected elementary school teacher and son of a Lutheran minister, who was preparing a geography lesson on Africa at the time and felt the need of direct tribal contact. We sat beside a prominent Chinese restaurateur (George Seto) who sported a bow tie and opera glasses. Our fathers had warned us both not to attend, and we were thankful not to be seated beside them.

The curtains parted on a darkened stage spotted with what appeared to be large mounds of grass. Upon a primal scream the grass sat up and started drumming — loud, primitive, sensual. The girls floated in on orange and purple floods and danced around the drummers in a frenzy. "Hypnotic and riveting," the *Galt Reporter* said the next day. They certainly did rivet. But it wasn't sleazy. The spark jumped, and people who had never shouted "Bravo" shouted "Bravo!" There were standing ovations. We had bitten the apple.

After the performance, I asked Len Iseler if he found the bare breasts disturbing, and he said to his own amazement that he was so caught up in the artistry that he scarcely noticed them, though he had to admit they were there. My experience was the same, and we wondered how we might sneak into another performance to better appreciate what we had missed.

The Ballet African was a cosmopolitan turn for Galt. Delicatessens opened and European cafés with decent-tasting bread appeared. The Salvation Army disappeared from the corner of Mill and Main, the Capitol packed the house again with the naughty revue *Oh, Coward!* and the Iroquois Hotel got a liquor licence.

47

The Foxy Lady

Soon the Foxy Lady took over the recently vacated Salvation Army citadel on Adam Street in Hespeler within a cry for help from the town hall police station. Again the clergy frothed and letters to the editor raged so that the Foxy Lady sold out every night. It was called "a cheap strip joint," and I and my friend Len Iseler went up to see for sure.

For reasons I can't recall we were in the company of two ladies. Probably because the price of admission was less than that at the Capitol Theatre. The place was packed well before curtain time with what appeared to be a meeting of the United Auto Workers. One other lady was there, wearing a corn cap. In the back row, as conspicuous as sausages on a white plate, sat two dapper plainclothes officers from the Ontario Provincial Police morality squad, feigning solemnity and jotting classified notes on pads held on their knees. Actually, it was Hespeler's chief of police, Fred Stewart, aided by the Kitchener morality squad, who finally busted the place, but the OPP were on hand just to take in the show.

To avoid pandemonium no alcohol was allowed on the premises. Nevertheless the place smelled like a beer parlour from which most of the patrons had come. Oddly, but undeniably cosmopolitan, both public lavatories were onstage, ladies to the left, gents to the right.

The performance, following a call for calm from the master of ceremonies who was also the principal male dancer, began when he lowered the needle arm of a Seabreeze portable record player perched to one side on a spoked wooden chair. As I recall, the first number was "Caravan." Two young ladies, one plump and the other skinny, burst from the wings and began flat-footed pirouettes that raised puffs of dust into the floodlights. There must have been a lighting man backstage, because the spots changed to red and green, the cue for the male dancer, dressed as an Arabian knight, to abandon the Seabreeze and stagger around clutching at the ladies' veils. The ladies, coyly batting their eyes and flashing their teeth, teased the knight, their leaping from his clutches causing "Caravan" on the Seabreeze to skip a few beats. One by one, tediously dragged out, the leering knight snatched off all the veils until, if you squinted in the dim light, you could see that the ladies were down to lace panties and bras. A chorus of men hollered, "Turn up the lights."

That was it for "Caravan," and the dance team, kicking the veils offstage, retired to prepare for the next offering. During the pause, a burly man wearing a hockey jacket mounted the stage to go to the lavatory. After he came out and the catcalls died down, the Seabreeze, sounding now like a mocha band, let fly with a wild Hungarian dance, and the ladies spun onstage in diaphanous nightgowns. The male dancer, still the Arabian knight, eyes blazing and panting with lust, tore after them. Now there was physical contact. They bumped bums as he ripped their gowns off. Again the ladies were left spinning in their panties and bras. After one more forgettable number, a man yelled, "Is that it?"

That was it, and the crowd, muttering disappointment, stomped back to the beer parlours.

Within days, satisfied the performance was corrupting citizens, the police closed the Foxy Lady forever. But the days weren't far off when ladies at the Sulphur Springs Hotel, the Travellers, and the Mirage Nightclub would, stark naked, choreograph gynecology and on special nights wrestle the patrons in foot-deep vats of green Jell-O, ranking us on the world stage with Calcutta and Amsterdam.

48

Preston Hastens the Decline

The Sulphur Springs Hotel, next door to the matronly clean Kress House in Preston, featured table-hopping prostitutes biked up from Toronto and a lot of local talent onstage. The night I was there with Len Iseler, Nancy Palmer started her dance just as we came in. Nancy was a local lady in her early twenties with a lovely face, beguiling smile, and knockout body. She was also deeply interested in spiritualism. An entrepreneur, she ran a rooming house for a biker club close to the Preston sewage treatment plant.

Nancy put a quarter in the jukebox onstage (as all the dancers had to do to ring up their theme songs), and after a recorded introduction from a Woodstock radio announcer, went into her dance. Bikers quit playing pool to watch. At the end of her number the Woodstock announcer said, "A big hand for Nancy Palmer, ladies and gentlemen ... a real big hand." And the patrons rose to applaud. Costume over her arm, she joined Leonard and me at our table.

The next girl up looked as if she had stepped off a school bus. Indeed, Leonard said, "She's one of my former pupils from St. Andrews," and he coughed up her name. She spotted him midway through her dance and tossed a few bumps our way. As soon as she finished, and while the applause still raged, she hopped straight to our table, naked, and with hands on her hips said, "Mr. Iseler, sir, what on earth are you doing in a dump like this?"

Leonard bought her a drink. "I'm glad to see that your pimples have all cleared up," he said.

The Sulphur, as it was affectionately known, had an electric ambience, and one was always braced for the outbreak of violence or possibly a fire. An American Vietnam War veteran compared the Sulphur favourably to a club in Saigon. Fire finally levelled the hotel. The newspapers said it was arson.

49

Sin on the Golden Mile

The Travellers Motor Inn on Hespeler Road had featured nude dancers for several years before the gala opening of the classy Mirage Nightclub directly across the street. But for some reason this new club riled the members of the moral majority more than anything since the Ballet African, and they mustered a pray-in picket line of mothers with children hoisting placards on sticks. "Toot if you hate sin," the placards said, and motorists tooted gleefully and waved. It rained, and a nearby restaurant sent out coffee and soft drinks to the line, which went round and round like a dead march. Hymns were sung.

Inevitably, the pickets turned their condemnation also on the Travellers and halted four lanes of tooting traffic as they crossed the road. I was covering the event for the *Reporter* and spoke with some of the protesters. Len Iseler was with me. A tall and burly Teutonic man who resembled Otto von Bismarck walked the line beside his wife. "Any man," he growled, "who likes to watch women dance naked has got to be sick." Leonard pressed a palm to his forehead to check for fever.

The invitation from the Mirage to watch ladies wrestle patrons in vats of Jell-O was too much to resist. Len Iseler was out of town, so I went with Bob Milne, a jazz bass fiddle player who had once accompanied Moe Koffman but had gone all wrong and inexplicably wound up suited and vested in the offices of Gore Mutual Insurance. He had just retired from Gore and wanted to rediscover his old roots in the squalor of nightlife. Milne was convinced that by the year 2000, five years down the road, civilization would end, so why not sin with abandon now and start praying for forgiveness fast in 1999?

The Jell-O wrestling didn't start until after midnight, so we had to while away an hour in the main lounge watching ladies on the runway demonstrate the largesse of Dow Corning's silicone breast implant sales staff. We sat beneath an electric printout sign that kept flashing the message "Secret closet lingerie shop now located behind our bar."

A petite and pretty non-silicone lady in a Budweiser bikini tried to sell us tickets to the Jell-O wrestling for $1. "There's a draw," she said, "and the winner gets to wrestle me." She couldn't have weighed more than 100 pounds. I declined for fear she might beat me, but a man beside me bought ten. Milne bought two, one for each of us, though I kept pushing mine back at him.

The wrestling pit was in an adjoining room full of billiard tables, several of which had been pushed aside and covered with plastic wraps. It was a small pit, about nine feet by nine feet, a wading pool really, flooded with eight inches of shimmering green Jell-O. Before the draw for the lucky contestant, Milne handed me both tickets, and I stuffed them down one of the hollow ring posts roping off the pit. Dozens of other tickets were already jammed down there.

The winner of the first draw, a stocky young buck with a Canadian flag tattooed on his chest, had to take on a tall husky girl with a formidable testosterone level wearing shorts and a T-shirt. They thrashed about so that the Jell-O hit the ceiling and plastered the industrial baseball team behind which Milne and I were hiding. She won.

Next, the pretty little lady who sold us the tickets took on the second draw winner, a runt of a man about my size who slipped on his first lunge and fell flat on his face. She sat on him and pitched handfuls of Jell-O with abandon in every direction. Someone pushed the referee into the pit, and she took him on, too. When the baseball team ran for cover, Milne and I took shelter under a billiard table.

"What on earth are we doing here?" I hollered over the lascivious howls. "We're senior citizens in our golden years."

"There's no time for golden years," Milne yelled back. "The end of civilization is right now!" Next he got the notion that a police raid was imminent, and we made hastily for the exit on our hands and knees.

Erika Kubassek was right.

50

Liberated Breasts

The moral degeneracy spilled out of the strip joints and threatened to engulf God-fearing citizens on the streets. A well-endowed (and not by Corning) University of Guelph student, Gwen Jacobs, paraded what she called her "liberated breasts" along a Guelph main street and got herself arrested. Her court case set fire to platoons of liberated breasts throughout the region, and they decided to defy the law with a topless demonstration in Waterloo Park.

Their parade presented a strange sight for people feeding the ducks. Two dozen news photographers retreated backwards in front of the women, shouting obscenities as they bumped one another, zoom lenses and microphones extended as they tripped down the path and over a narrow wooden footbridge, at times perilous inches ahead of the wobbling bare breasts of Adele Arnold, a middle-aged Cambridge woman who was carrying the flag. Several hundred feminists followed, chanting, waving placards, and threatening to rip off their blouses at any moment.

"Keep your laws off our breasts," the women chanted as they headed for the police hiding behind their cruisers by the tennis courts. When the police pounced on Adele Arnold, wrapped her in a blanket, and pushed her into a cruiser, the chant changed to "Let her go, let her go." It reached a fearsome pitch. Men joined in. More tops came off, more arrests. One comely girl danced bare-breasted atop a cruiser until a female officer grabbed her by the ankle and dragged her off. Men and women lay on the road to prevent the cruisers from moving.

A new chant started: "The law's got my body." A distant storm over Cambridge added its thunder. The melee jammed up between the duck pond and the tennis court bubble. Sonia Provost Derbecker climbed atop the bubble's retaining wall and breast-fed her baby, Katrina, in plain view. A short boy, about ten years old, stood on the crossbar of his bicycle to get a better view. A powerful-looking woman with freckles on her biceps pushed him off. "Don't stare, you little bastard!" she shouted. "It's rude."

The media, cameras clicking, bulbs flashing, swept to and fro like a flock of starlings. They came from everywhere — CBC, CTV, *Toronto Star*, all the big guys. Michael Lambert from the European Press Agency was there. His office in Paris learned of the upcoming demonstration from the wire service and dispatched him from Montreal. Two weeks earlier he was covering the civil war in Armenia.

The main corps of women broke free of the police and paraded back over the wooden bridge past the ducks again, chanting, "Our breasts are not obscene." The ducks quacked back. Now the parade headed to police headquarters on Erb Street beside the park, led by a police cruiser with its siren and flashing lights on.

Gwen Jacobs, who had bared her breasts in Guelph, was now fully clothed as she waited on the police station steps to make a speech. The police, determined to shield us from the sight of what we fed on when we were babies, stood sternly behind her. More police, including the chief, peered out the station windows. A plainclothes officer balanced on a window ledge to photograph the press photographing him. Every time he raised his video camera his service revolver stuck out from under his jacket and the crowd howled. Fearing that his fly was open, he climbed down and went inside. A few gay rights activists, one with steel rings piercing his nipples and pink hair, and a dapper little man wearing only a turquoise jockstrap, tried in vain to get arrested. Their placard said Why Not Us?

"Get lost," a policeman said, "this is just tits."

51

The Good Guys Gangbuster Pickett

In spite of our general moral collapse, officers of the law soldiered on with courage, humility, meagre resources, and low pay to keep drunks off the streets and see that they were humanely treated. In Hespeler they were well fed, and in Ayr they were entertained.

Before regional government standardized law and order, outposts such as Hespeler and Ayr had to make due with the Ten Commandments and whatever manpower and facilities a tight budget would allow. Chief Tom Wilson in Hespeler, for instance, had a jail but no police cruiser. Chief Cecil Pickett in Ayr had a cruiser but no jail. And they were too far apart to share resources.

Indeed, Ayr had no police force at all until, back in the 1940s, Ulysses Lauzon and Mickey MacDonald held up the Bank of Commerce there and ran off with $100,000. They were never caught, though years later Lauzon's bullet-riddled body was discovered in a Florida turpentine swamp. Bank robberies, which today are a bit boring, were exciting events back then. The Royal Family hadn't become unhinged yet, and so bank robberies still made the front pages.

After the Ayr robbery, villages everywhere realized how vulnerable they were to big-city gangsters and cried out to the Ontario Provincial Police for protection. Ayr went a step farther and founded its own police force, which consisted of Cecil Pickett, a big, jovial, trusted, and well-liked native of the village.

Now that he's gone he's become a legendary figure involved in the most improbable events. Soon after his ordination as village constable, so the story goes, he was assigned to paint the angle parking lines at the cenotaph square and painted them backwards so that they had to be scrubbed off with a wire brush and redone. And a Halloween deputy he hired to control the local kids was abducted and tied to a tree in a field.

Pickett was also the small animal control officer and ticketed anyone who failed to buy a dog licence. Villagers raised a row when they learned the chief didn't have a licence for his own dog, a stately black retriever that, I believe, he called Pluto. Pickett claimed that a police dog with Pluto's responsibilities didn't need a licence, but the villagers insisted that no dog was above the law, and the chief was forced to buy him a licence. Two weeks later Pluto died of old age.

I remember Pluto in his prime. He was always at the chief's side and was an inspiration to see in action. Occasionally, I played drums in a dance band in Reid's Hall on Northumberland Street. The dances were straitlaced and sober, and Chief Pickett always dropped in to make sure they stayed that way. Pluto came into the hall with him to have a sniff. Cecil claimed the dog could smell alcohol upwind. Like his master, the dog was good-natured and sociable, and everyone fussed over him as he walked, wagging his tail, along the stag line.

That night he stopped to sniff a man slumped in a chair. Sure enough, the man was drunk and law and order ensued. Chief Pickett, with the help of many hands, hoisted the drunk to his feet and eased him out the door to the cruiser. It was intermission, and out of curiosity I joined the spectators outside. The chief shouldered the man onto the rear seat of the cruiser, and Pluto, without being ordered, hopped in beside him. As the cruiser pulled away, I could see the man's head lolling against the window, and Pluto's noble silhouette beside him, straight as a general and a role model for licensed dogs everywhere. I asked a man standing there where the chief was taking his prisoner, since I understood that he had no jail. "Oh, Cecil," the man said, "he'll just take him home to watch the hockey game. He likes company."

He was known as Gangbuster Pickett. There were no more bank robberies in Ayr.

52
The Royal Hespeler Constabulary

As a boy in Ireland, George Woods was fascinated with the great police forces of the world such as Scotland Yard and the Royal Irish Constabulary. In 1921, at age fifteen, when he moved with his parents to Canada, he hoped to see the Royal Canadian Mounted Police in action. Imagine his amazement when he landed in Hespeler and found that the town's total police force consisted of Chief Tom Wilson with no visible means of transportation.

George said that Chief Wilson never owned or drove a car. Now and then he had to deputize someone to drive him to the scene of a crime, but it was seldom more than a couple of blocks away — easy walking distance. Usually, he found criminals within arm's reach. Many of them were merely drunks or transients in search of a dry cell and a good meal. Indeed some of them turned themselves in because they liked the chief's stew. He kept a large pot of stew brewing in the furnace room adjacent to the jail cells in the basement of the town hall and fed it free of charge to the inmates. They took turns stirring it and pitched in to cut up the meat and vegetables that the chief scrounged from local grocery stores and butcher shops. George wondered if any of the pieces ever made it to the bottom of the pot. The stew comforted hundreds of empty stomachs, especially in winter.

William Woods, George's father, started a cartage business in Hespeler (the forerunner of Woods Transport) and employed his son as a driver. When Woods Taxi Service came into being, utilizing the family car, young George was assigned to drive it and soon found himself a part-time deputy of Chief Wilson. In those days, George said, you learned to drive first and got your licence whenever it was convenient.

One Saturday night he got a call to meet the chief in front of the Odd Fellows Hall on Queen Street where some rowdies from Guelph were disrupting a dance. By the time he got to the hall, the chief had already strong-armed the gang leader to the curb. The man was burly, truculent, and drunk, and flailed wildly about while George held the cab door open like a chauffeur and the chief heaved the troublemaker into the back seat. The chief got in beside the prisoner, and the two wrestled all the way to the jail, fortunately just the usual two blocks distant. There the miscreant held on to the car's door frame so that the chief couldn't drag him out.

"Rap his knuckles!" the chief hollered.

George grabbed a heavy wrench and gave the man's knuckles a rap. He howled and let go, and the chief marched him in an arm lock to the basement jail where George, again like a chauffeur, held open the door. There the prisoner broke free, and the three of them nearly pitched down the stairs. But Chief Wilson never lost his cool. He withdrew from his hip pocket his trusty "cosh" and slugged the man behind the ear. A cosh was a leather pouch full of lead shot, a sort of blackjack. The cosh had a calming effect on the man, and he co-operated fully while George and the chief dragged him on his back across the floor and tossed him into a cell and onto an iron cot.

Although the chief's jacket was torn, brass buttons had flown off, and his shins were black and blue, he didn't seem at all perturbed. In fact, George said, he wasn't even breathing hard. He just sat at his desk and jotted down some notes. When the prisoner regained consciousness and sobered up, he didn't call his lawyer or his mother or Amnesty International. He took his turn stirring the chief's stew for a while and then sat down with a couple of other inmates to eat it.

Chief Tom Wilson wasn't one of the great police forces of the world, but he kept pretty good law and order in Hespeler for more than forty years.

53

Heartbreaking Arrest

*C*hief Tom Wilson's toughest job was to arrest and charge with murder the man who had saved the lives of two of his sons, one of those improbable Hespeler epics that illustrate how there the Lord certainly worked in strange ways.

As Tom Wilson, Jr., tells it, in 1932 he and his two brothers and three sisters lived with their parents in an old two-storey house on Queen Street. The house was owned by Dominion Woollens and Worsteds and was rented to Tom's father. For reasons lost to time their house was to be moved from Queen up a hill to the road above now called Tannery Street. The contractor, who was drunk much of the time, got the house only halfway up the hill and plunked it onto a vacant lot. No one seemed to mind this, and the Wilsons moved in.

There was a gravel pit above Tannery Street where young Tom, age three, and his brothers began to play. They dug caves under laminations of sand. One day a cave collapsed and buried Tom and his brother, Rody, age seven. Fortunately, the third brother, Donald, thirteen, was standing clear of the cave-in and ran hollering for help down the hill.

A family named White lived next door to the Wilsons, and Tom said they were the best neighbours you could ever hope to have. Especially, that day, because young Reg White was digging in his garden when Donald ran by sounding the alarm. Reg hotfooted up the hill and dug the boys out just in time. Tom, dusting the sand off his sun suit, didn't consider it a big deal, even though he was a minute away from suffocating to death. He was more concerned about a nickel he had lost. Brother Rody had lost a red toy car.

To the Wilsons, indeed to the whole town, Reg became an instant hero, which proved to be a badly needed lift to his self-esteem. He was what today we would call intellectually challenged and the butt of cruel jokes. Perhaps twenty years old at the time, Reg was in love with a girl who grew up in the Children's Aid Orphanage on Guelph Street and worked in town as a domestic. She, too, was intellectually challenged, but they made a good pair and in time decided to get married.

Reg had been working on a farm for an elderly couple named Milroy who lived on a cul-de-sac off Branchton Road close to Galt. They owed Reg several hundred dollars for the work he had done, a lot of money then, and one morning he went there to collect. He needed the cash right away because he was in a hurry to get married. When the Milroys told him they couldn't pay all at once, Reg, whose sole fault was a terrible temper, killed them with an axe.

At first no one suspected him, but an incriminating remark he let slip in George Sim's poolroom the next day sent George straight to Chief Tom. The chief said it shook him to his boots to have to arrest, charge with murder, and lead to jail in handcuffs the man who had saved his two sons and who was practically a member of the family. It shook him further when he was obliged to witness Reg's hanging in the Kitchener jail yard. Reg was the last man to be hanged there.

White readily pleaded guilty, and Ray Myers, his defence counsel, recounted Reg's childlike redemption just minutes from the gallows. A Salvation Army chaplain tried to comfort the condemned man in his cell. After his confession, Reg repeatedly repented and desperately sought forgiveness. The chaplain said not to worry, that he had suffered enough for his crime and God would surely hear his pleas for mercy and grant it. What's more, he would go to heaven and meet the Milroys.

Reg's face brightened. "Meet the Milroys?"

The chaplain assured him that the Milroys would be there, and being good Christians, they would forgive him.

"And will you come to heaven, too?" he asked the chaplain.

"Certainly, someday," the chaplain replied.

Reg stood and shook the chaplain's hand. "Well, then," he said, smiling, "we'll see you there."

Shortly after, the hood was put over Reg's head.

Mr. Myers said he didn't mind losing a case when everyone involved went to heaven.

And who knows who Reg met up there? The Milroys were cousins of Millicent Milroy whose tombstone in Galt's Mountview Cemetery states that she was the morganatic wife of Edward VIII, prince of Wales, and king of England until he ran off with Wallis Simpson. Surely, Millicent and Edward are in heaven and possibly even Wallis, though the jury is still out on her friend Hitler. I'll let you know in a few years. No one can say what happened to Reg's fiancée.

Young Tom Wilson, saved by Reg from certain death in the gravel pit, grew up to become a special investigator for the federal income tax department. Three cheers for Reg White!

54
Safety Joe McCabe

After Constable Joe McCabe busted his kneecap on a sidewalk in Galt while helping to subdue a violent offender in the 1950s, people said his days on the police force were over. They were wrong.

Not long afterwards I asked Galt's chief of police, Clare Kunkle, who, hypothetically, he would assign to protect me if my life were threatened (it wasn't then, but it is now). Without hesitation he said, "Joe McCabe."

"How's that?" I asked. "Joe has a busted knee."

"He would only have to stand beside you," Kunkle said. "No one will attack a friend of Joe McCabe."

Joe was held in such high esteem that he would have made a great pope — if only he hadn't had twelve children. Children, everybody's children, loved him. He was Santa Claus all year. And that was the main reason Chief Kunkle assigned him to be safety officer for the city's public schools. His job was to visit elementary classrooms and discuss the dangers of thin ice, riding bicycles backwards, and throwing snowballs at seniors or policemen. Joe often showed movies illustrating these dangers.

A teacher at Blair Road School, Mrs. Cathy Iseler (the second of Len Iseler's three wives), recounted one of Joe's more memorable lessons.

Whenever she told her grade four class that Constable McCabe was coming, the kids would cheer and watch eagerly out the window for the sight of his car. That day, however, Joe was delivered in a police cruiser. Due to an act of God in which Joe's auto collided with the side of an Ontario Provincial Police officer's house, the constable's driver's licence was under suspension and he had to be chauffeured to his safety lectures. The kids were thrilled, because they assumed he had gotten a promotion. They rose as he entered and said as always, "Good morning, Mr. McCabe."

"Good morning, boys and girls," Joe replied as always.

After a few words about the dangers of roller skating on gravel and the need to check and double-check every lock and light switch in the house, Joe set up his projector, had the blinds pulled, and asked someone to turn off the lights. The half-hour film was full of things the kids loved: people falling down stairs, banging their thumbs with hammers, and setting fire to their houses. When the lights came back on, Joe looked down at a pile of coiled film rising two feet off the floor. He had forgotten to attach the film to the rewind reel. Mrs. Iseler lugged the projector out to the cruiser, and Joe carried the pile of film.

"Goodbye, Mr. McCabe," the kids said in unison.

"Goodbye, boys and girls," Joe replied. "See you again soon and take care."

Joe was a great teacher, not just because he held the complete trust of the kids but because he taught by example.

55

Len Gaudette — Another Good Guy

When Albert Lamond retired as the Galt Arena's manager in 1959 after thirty-six years of impeccable service, it was no easy task to fill his shoes. He was an able and honest administrator —

conservative, sedate, a gentleman. So locals got nervous when he was replaced by a man named Len Gaudette, a loose cannon who had instigated some of the most bizarre stunts seen in arenas anywhere.

Len played the villainous Black Eagle in a British ice show starring Barbara Ann Scott, "Rose Marie on Ice," back in the 1940s, and then ran off to play hockey in Switzerland. They said he was nuts. They were right. He was nuts, but he wasn't stupid. He was a complex man who loved sports, circuses, Spike Jones, country and western music, animals, people, and fun, irreverent one minute and moralistic the next.

One of the first things he did at the Galt Arena was to discourage the ladies from defacing the washroom walls with vulgar messages in lipstick by painting the walls lipstick red. Then he got the arena hopping. He brought in the Grand Ole Opry with Grandpa Jones, Big Slim, and Hank Snow; wrestling with Whipper Billy Watson and Lord Athol Layton; the Garden Brothers' Circus with Buffalo Bill; and hockey ... from nothing to the Allan Cup in two years. Residents of Shade Street began to complain about parking congestion. Arena crowds parked bumper to bumper from Soper Park to Main Street.

To get hockey started, Gaudette formed a Senior B team, climbed into a uniform, and played on a line himself. And he found time to do a duo clown act with the Galt Figure Skating Club, which had on its roster the then young Toller Cranston. The other clown skating with him was the ever-young Len Iseler.

He promoted roller and ice skating whenever the hockey and circus crowds left parking space. People skated to Ken Hurst on the organ and danced to the Jay Rockers, a surging local group that Gaudette was promoting on the side. And who can forget the Grand March on Roller Skates — eight abreast down the centre of the rink led by Tink Clark with a baton?

Tuesday night it was boxing starring such household names as Sam Pernick and Punchy Proctor from the Galt Board of Works. If a referee failed to show, Gaudette refereed. If a boxer failed to appear, he phoned the Royal Hotel. One night the Royal dispatched its champion heavyweight bartender and bouncer, Wally Balaban, to fill in. Wally came with a cheering section of close to forty from the beer parlour. He said he would fight only if they got in free. They did. The fight lasted one punch.

Wally hadn't bothered to warm up. His fans, cheering and singing as if he had won, left him flat on the canvas and marched back to the Royal.

Gaudette himself never boxed. As we noted, he was nuts but not stupid. He was the P.T. Barnum of Shade Street.

56

The Piano Marathon

*L*en Gaudette was a very caring man who looked out for his friends and gave a lot of money to the Humane Society. When he was managing the arena in Aylmer, before he came to Galt, he helped a friend launch a career in music. Guy Bastien, stationed at the Royal Canadian Air Force base close by, was unhappy in the military and wanted out but didn't have another line of work to turn to. However, he played the piano quite well, and Gaudette thought that doing something sensational with this talent could launch him into a career in show business. He talked Bastien into trying to break the world piano marathon record. Desperate for a change in his lifestyle, Bastien agreed to give it a try. Gaudette supplied the piano and a banquet hall above the arena.

So it was that on a hot day in July 1955, people passing the Aylmer Arena in the morning heard a piano tinkling upstairs. When they passed again at 5:00 p.m., it was still tinkling. That night residents close to the arena sat on their front porches and listened to the tinkling until bedtime. Pleasant listening for a summer night, all the old standards: "Sunny Side of the Street," "Blue Moon," "The Rose of Tralee." Not until the citizens listened to the tinkling as they lay in bed did they begin to wonder who was doing it. All night the piano tinkled, and in the morning children sneaked through a door left open and up the stairs to the hall. Gaudette arrived and handed out a pile of sandwiches.

The children told their parents about the man onstage who couldn't stop playing the piano. Word spread, and soon a reporter from the *St. Thomas Times-Journal* came to see for himself. There was Guy Bastien onstage at an old upright Baldwin piano, hollow-eyed and wan but smiling and playing requests. Occasionally, Gaudette came on to spoon-feed the man, hold water to his lips, and mop his brow. And on cue he drew a curtain so that Bastien, with a minimum of humiliation, could urinate through a hookup of pipes and bottles. The spectators remained decently quiet while this went on, even though the piano went out of metre and gave way to some bad chords. They applauded with restraint each time the curtain opened again.

By now reporters from the *London Free Press* and the *Toronto Star* were on hand, and Gaudette set up a lunch counter and hired a four-piece band. Bastien played along with the band, and on Saturday night they performed for a dance. Gaudette put his mother-in-law on the door to collect the 50 cent admission and keep her out of his hair.

Everyone was pulling for Bastien. Telegrams arrived from distant friends and relatives who had heard about the marathon on the news. Gaudette read them to the crowd between numbers. "Keep going, Guy. Stop," the telegrams said, and Gaudette told Bastien to ignore the "stops." The local barber turned out to massage Bastien's neck and back with a vibrator to ease the cramps and keep his circulation going. By 10:00 p.m., however, all but three of his fingers were paralyzed. He had been playing for fifty-eight straight hours and was beginning to drool and nod off. The St. John's Ambulance crew was nodding off, too.

At 11:00 p.m. Gaudette, sensing a terminal event, removed the compress from Bastien's head and spoke into his ear. "Guy," he said, "don't listen to me or the crowd. You just do whatever you wish to do."

At those words Bastien collapsed into an alarming chord and rolled off his stool and onto the floor. The St. John's Ambulance crew awoke and, smiling for the first time, leaped into action. They disconnected Bastien from his pipes and bottles and rushed him off to the hospital in St. Thomas. The band played "Knees Up Mother Brown," and the crowd gave Guy a standing ovation. He hadn't broken the world record, but he had played fifty-nine tortured hours. After a night in the hospital, Bastien headed straight home for Quebec.

"I visited him in the hospital," Len Gaudette said later, "but I haven't seen him since. I don't know why he hasn't answered my letters, though, after all I did for him."

57

The Wooden-Legged Goaltender

In 1948 Len Gaudette coached the Fort William Rovers senior hockey team on an exhibition tour through Northern Ontario. The Rovers were beating every opponent, and one night they were humbling a club in Schreiber for the third consecutive game. The Rovers led 8–1 going into the last period, and the crowd, getting bored and restless, was eyeing the exits. Nothing, it seemed, short of a late brawl could make the game worth watching to the end. Gaudette changed all that.

A good friend of Len's, let's call him Art, a goaltender of great promise before the war, had come along on the team bus. He couldn't play goal anymore because he had lost a leg in the navy, but he still lived hockey and travelled everywhere with the Rovers. "Len," Art often said, "I'd give anything to be out in that net again."

So that night, with his team ahead 8–1 in the third period and beyond defeat, Gaudette decided to make Art a happy man. He got him into the spare goaltender's suit and put him in the net. "I'll always remember this, Len," Art said as he left the bench. So would everybody else.

No one except the Rovers knew about Art's wooden leg. The spectators must have wondered, though, why Gaudette would replace a red-hot goaltender with one who had to be carried to the net and who had to support himself with his left arm on the top of the crossbar.

The Rovers, of course, ferociously defended Art so that for a long time there wasn't a shot on his net. Five minutes from the end, however, a Schreiber forward got a breakaway. Art removed his arm from the crossbar, took the classic goaltender's crouch , and fixed his eyes on the puck. The Schreiber player feinted to the left and then suddenly shifted to the right. Art shifted suddenly, too. That was when his leg flew off and slid across the ice. Artificial limbs weren't as sophisticated then as they are now. The man on the breakaway forgot to shoot the puck, the crowd stood in shock, and Gaudette bowed his head. Two teammates carried Art back to the bench. A linesman followed with his leg.

By now the regular Rovers goaltender was sitting in the dressing room in his shorts drinking beer. He had had three or four and was getting boisterous. Gaudette didn't want to treat the crowd to the sight of another goaltender being carried out to the net, so he put a defenceman in goal for the remaining minutes.

"Art took it all with his usual good humour," Gaudette said later. "He was a 100 percent good sport. And to this day he must be proud of being the only goaltender in the record books who stopped a breakaway by throwing his leg at it. Strange, though, he's another guy who never answers my letters."

58

Incidental Disasters — Hazel

We had a few disasters to distract us from our struggle between good and evil. Hurricane Hazel, for instance.

Hazel rolled up from Haiti and the Carolinas in October 1954 and collided with a cold front over Toronto, unloading more than eight inches of rain. Galt got five. The next morning, Saturday, was sunny and bright and made the rain of the previous day seem like a bad dream. I dropped down to Connie McFadyen's record store on Water Street to listen to the Toronto news on the radio. Eighty-one people had died there, but here we were high and dry.

Connie sent her assistant out for coffee. No sooner had she stepped out the door than she popped back in again to say that coffee was running down the gutter. We all ran out to see, and sure enough there was a stream the colour of coffee with cream added rushing past the curb. It was whipping past the curb on the far side of the street, too, and people were peering at it, their eyes following the bubbles and sticks drifting by. The surge had appeared suddenly, without warning, and rose at an alarming rate. A man hammered on the back door of the store and stuck his head in to say that water was sweeping down the back lane and that Connie had better move her car. Evidently, the deluge of the previous day had just begun to raise the Grand River. By the time Connie got to her Buick behind her shop, she was up to her ankles in water.

I ran the half block to the corner of Main and Water, the four banks as we called it, in time to see a two-inch-thick steel storm drain in front of the Bank of Commerce rise up on a boil of brown water and slide off onto the road. The storm drains began to hemorrhage flood water. I didn't have a car and walked briskly up to Main and Ainslie where Briscoe's Department Store was in crisis. Employees in the basement were desperately loading merchandise onto tables above the rising murk. Suddenly, the outside stairwell door burst in and unleashed a swirling brown torrent. The last man to reach the steps leading upstairs, I was told, had to swim. In minutes the water was up to the basement ceiling. This scene was repeated in every store basement south of Ainslie, and it was amazing that no one drowned.

The worst part of the flood was the cleanup. Stores such as Briscoe's, Fraser Hardware, and Wilson's Drapery were clotted with muck and debris, the merchandise ruined. Little of it was insured. Only people living on high hills could get flood insurance, and even those premiums were high. All the houses on south Water Street were full of the same stinking mire through all their downstairs rooms right up to the window ledges. They had to be hosed out.

Water flooded the Capitol Theatre halfway up the aisles from the stage and presented the manager, Eddy Landsborough, with an odd problem. The colour in the long aisle carpets up to the water line had run and turned from deep purple to pink. But it didn't look bad. Trouble was only half the length of each carpet had gotten soaked. Eddie, noting how expensive it would be to have them replaced, decided to stick with the new colour. In an attempt to match up the old colour with the new, he had the carpets hauled down to the river and the dry ends soaked for hours. No luck. The dyes wouldn't run. Men jumped on them and attacked them with toilet plungers, but only the muddy flood waters seemed to have the magic.

Phil Pratt, whose moving vans were a pillar of society in those days, got a job hauling flood-ruined footwear from a shoe store to the dump. He hired a helper recommended by the employment office. When they got to the dump, his assistant brushed off a bundle he had spirited out of a dry part of the store and held up a brand-new pair of undamaged boots. Stolen! Pratt was mortified. But justice was dealt. They were both lefts.

59

Punished for Rejecting Billy Graham

$\mathcal{I}$, still can't pass the corner of East Main Street and Highway 8 without remembering the Highway Garage, that service centre shaped like the Rock of Gibraltar but with the facade of an old English cottage that towered over the intersection for decades. My parents referred to it as the "tollgate" because there used to be one there.

When we were kids and there was a big snowstorm, we would ski up East Main at night to see if the highway was closed. We would stand across from the Highway Garage and squint through the sleet towards Hamilton and wait for the headlights of cars trying to make it through. Anyone who did went straight into the warm harbour of the Highway Garage lunch-room, batting the snow from their coats and hollering with relief.

The lunchroom was a classy place to go when you were a teenager. You could smoke and mingle with travellers and fill up your bicycle tires outside with free air. Galt met the world there. Famous jazz bands like Andy Kirk and His Clouds of Joy stopped there for gas and food on their way to the Summer Gardens in Kitchener. Ulysses Lauzon and Mickey MacDonald stopped there for lunch on their way to rob the Bank of Commerce in Ayr of $100,000.

It wasn't dull upstairs, either. One day in the 1940s my mother pulled her copy of Hush Weekly from under the cushion on the Morris chair in our kitchen and showed me front-page photos of the provincial police leading men and girls to the police wagon outside the Highway Garage. The men, prominent local businessmen, of course, covered their faces with their fedoras, and the girls stuck their tongues out. "Just go to the lunchroom," Mom said. "Not upstairs." The night he won the raving mad federal by-election of 1964, Max Saltsman and his campaign manager, Bob Kerr, fled the victory celebration and walked to the Highway Garage just for peace and quiet and a cheese sandwich.

The Highway Garage ceased to be the last outpost when the big plazas surrounded it in the 1960s — Steinberg's to the north and the Grand Valley Discount Centre to the south.

I digress now to a disaster of no interest to anyone except my sister, Shirley, and me. The eighteen acres on which Steinberg's built their plaza belonged for many years to William Graham, a market gardener. He had an orchard of apples, peaches, pears, and cherries, but also a couple of acres of strawberries and raspberries, which my grandmother, Dinah Green, and I were eager to pick for a dollar a day. This was in the days before fruit and tobacco farmers began to import slave labour from the Caribbean.

Mr. Graham — Billy Graham we called him — was a devout Anglican long before his namesake was born and lived as a Christian should: no smoking, no drinking, and a lot of praying in the parlour during thunderstorms. He provided our family with free milk during the Great Depression, and it was my job to hike up to the farm after school and bring the milk home daily. It wasn't pasteurized, but no one in our family contracted tuberculosis, though three close relatives who drank pasteurized milk did.

Soon after the outbreak of World War II, Mr. Graham decided to retire. He offered my father first chance at buying his farm, barn, and cow, minus the house, for $1,800. I remember my parents discussing the offer at the kitchen table, and my mother saying, "What on earth would you do with eighteen acres and a cow? Shirley couldn't handle it, and Bob is hopeless. Stick with your job at the shoe factory." So they passed, someone else bought the land, and a few years later the land was sold to Steinberg's for $1 million.

128

60

The Discount Fire

In 1961 the Grand Valley Discount Centre, in a mall across the street from Steinberg's, was the Wal-Mart of its day, and thousands of shoppers flocked to the grand opening. Even more flocked to the grand closing one week later when it burned to the ground.

I happened by when the first fire truck was pulling up. It was November 18, just after 6:00 p.m., and dark. White smoke ghosted around the east end of the block-long store, but the lights were still on and 500 shoppers plodded towards the exits. There was a *Titanic*-like mentality. No one believed that this spanking new store could go. Incredibly, there were no fire hydrants on the property (still in North Dumfries), and firemen had to run a hose half a mile to the nearest hydrant on the corner of Main and Pine in the city.

The smoke turned ominously brown and, propelled by intense heat above a false ceiling, began to billow out from under the eaves. From the parking lot you could watch the whole length of the store like one long television set. The false ceiling at the east end dropped, and deep red flames licked down like a dragon's tongue. Suddenly, a front window blew out, the wind rushed in, and the flames rolled table loads of clothes through the air towards the staff who were now running for the exits with one arm in their coats. Still the lights were on. They went out briefly and came on again and then went out for keeps. Only then, when the flames provided all the light, did it become really frightening. At that point the parking lot became a madhouse of cars trying to escape the embers and not smash into one another.

You became aware of the awful sounds: the cascading crash of glass, ammunition exploding in the hardware section, monkeys and birds screeching in the pet department (the fish boiled in the only available water), the wailing of more and more sirens, and the boom of bullhorns wielded by policemen ordering onlookers to stand back. A turquoise Mini Minor, a raffle prize parked in front of the main entrance, caught fire and blew up. A white Cadillac sedan careened across the lot, tires screeching as it smashed into the brick wall at the west end of the building. It was Michele Martino, the plaza owner, hysterical with grief. He had to be led to safety, shouting and in tears.

My attention was drawn to a drama unfolding between a Ferris wheel and the blazing Mini Minor where a man was single-handedly dismantling a merry-go-round. He kept disappearing in billows of black smoke seeded with burning embers. But every time the smoke lifted, there he was, silhouetted against the flames, hammering and wrenching and racing with parts to his truck parked close by. The smoke would part, and there he would be running for his truck with a wooden horse. He would reappear, batting at embers on the merry-go-round awning. The crowd began to cheer, but I doubt if he heard them. In an astonishingly short time he dismantled the entire merry-go-round and drove off in his truck, leaving only the centre spindle.

The discount centre was a $2 million write-off but was rebuilt and reopened as the M & M Discount Centre, this time with hydrants and a sprinkler system. Nevertheless, after a brief spell of prosperity and a short term as a role model of fire safety, it, too, burned down. The nearby old Highway Garage wouldn't quit. It had to be torn down.

61

The Fireproof Inferno

For the first half of the twentieth century the Iroquois Hotel was the premier dining and convention centre in Galt. Its cuisine attracted diners from Kitchener. Its dining-room walls were adorned with original paintings by Homer Watson. John Diefenbaker, a rising young political star from the West, fired up the local Conservatives there in the late 1940s. Outside, a sign attached to a column of the portico declared that the food within was recommended by world-renowned gourmet Duncan Hines, and beneath that another sign invited everyone to "plan your next affair in our dining room."

The place had class, but during its last twenty-five years the merciless law of deterioration handed the hotel over to the termites, the proletariat, and the banks. The Playpen Lounge replaced what had been a more or less orderly beverage room.

For years the hotel was the editorial outpost of *Reporter* columnist Earl Werstine and the source of many of his stories. It was also the branch office of dentist Dr. Lorne Winter, who on occasion extracted teeth there free of charge. Back in the 1920s a local tightrope aerialist, Professor Cromwell, as he was billed (he had walked a wire across the Niagara Gorge), crossed Main Street on a wire stretched from the roof of the Iroquois to the roof of the Royal Hotel opposite, a feat exceeded only by those daredevils who made it from beer parlour to beer parlour through the traffic on their hands and knees.

The Playpen Lounge introduced rock bands, exotic dancers, a less-sophisticated clientele, and savage fights. During one of these fights, the Iroquois lost its last notable tenant, tattoo artist Painless Jeff Baker. While descending the stairs from his room to the main lobby, Jeff was hit over the head with a chair by a man chased out of the lounge. When released from the hospital, Jeff packed his bags and headed back to England. Canada was no longer safe, he said. That fight closed the lounge for two weeks for repairs. Clearly, the end was in sight. In 1974 the hotel was listed for sale four times.

On April 6, 1975, a Sunday, John Slee, a resident of room 53 on the third floor, awakened to pounding on his door. Kelly Klere, one of the new owners from Toronto, greeted him and told him that Regional Pest Control was on hand to fumigate the place and everyone had to vacate immediately. Robert Lunn, who played in the Playpen Lounge band, and Keith Robinson on the same floor were also alerted. In all twenty residents were ordered out.

Lunn went to feed some pigeons he kept behind a house on Beverly Street. He returned around 11:30 a.m. to see what he presumed to be fumigation fog wafting from the windows on the hotel's top floor. Police

Sergeant John Sindel, suspecting something more sinister, kicked in a locked rear door and was greeted by a burst of hot black smoke. The first firemen from the Dickson Street station a block away, Roy Turner, Robert Hughes, and Captain Tom Mercer, arrived two minutes after Sindel sounded the alarm at 11:47. They were there, along with every other available fireman, for the rest of the day. No amount of water could dampen the fire down.

Hordes of sightseers rushed down to watch the fire, now a regular Main Street event. A couple of Sundays earlier a fire just doors away from the Iroquois had gutted a textile warehouse above Howard's Gift Shop, ruining it in the process. On another Sunday the Neptune Seafood Restaurant, half a block down and next to Griffith's Sport Shop, suddenly turned into a furnace hot enough to melt the metal furniture.

Oddly, all the properties burned were connected to Jack Mamman of Montreal, the new owner of Centex Textiles on Dobbie Drive, the scene of at least four more mysterious fires within a year. Mamman didn't own the Iroquois but held the option to buy it and collect the fire insurance that had been doubled the week before, an option he dropped when the Ontario fire marshal declared arson. Rumours spread like the fires, especially after Eric Campbell, Iroquois Hotel manager Joe Burke's insurance agent, was killed in a mysterious car accident.

There were no more fires after Centex had its insurance cancelled, and Sundays in Galt became rather dull again. We might note that on the date of the fire, April 6, four inches of snow had fallen overnight and inebriates on the roof of the Royal Hotel pelted firemen with snowballs. The city purchased the Iroquois ruin for $175,000. The hotel was built in 1894 for $12,000 by George Bernhardt two years before the *Galt Reporter* published its first daily edition. Mr. Bernhardt had declared in the paper that his hotel had been "built to be strictly fireproof."

62

The Liberal Disaster

The South Waterloo Liberal Association suffered a disaster of biblical proportions during the 1964 federal by-election. There wasn't any fire or flood but a lot of locusts.

South Waterloo had been a Conservative stronghold since Confederation, lost only once to the Liberals during the 1950s when Arthur White gained the seat for one term. Gordon Chaplin succeeded Mr. White and became virtually invincible until he died in office in 1964. The by-election to fill his seat was called for November 3 of that year.

The Liberals formed the federal government, and Lester B. Pearson was prime minister. The flag debate had been raging for months, and little important legislation was passed while Pearson and Tory leader John Diefenbaker dickered over whether the flag should have one maple leaf or three. The public was in a frothing rage over the stalemate and was set to fire both barrels at both parties given the chance. The South Waterloo by-election presented the chance everyone was waiting for.

Rod Stewart, previously a strong candidate for the New Democratic Party, had become disenchanted with his local riding association and indicated he might return to the Liberals from whence he had come. When this aroma drifted to Ottawa, Liberal organizers Keith "The Rainmaker" Davey, Eric Strathdee, and Senator D.L. Lang, desperate to knock off a Tory stronghold, parachuted into Galt to convince Stewart that his prime minister needed him. Indeed they flew him to Ottawa for an audience with Pearson.

Reborn, Stewart agreed to run for the Liberals, and the organizers guaranteed him the nomination. They neglected, however, to check this out with the local nominating committee members, who favoured Donald McQueen Shaver, the loyal candidate who had run strongly in the riding twice before. They also overlooked the integrity of the chairman of that nominating committee, Carman Thornton, who suspected the nomination was being rigged when he learned that voting memberships were being sold to Stewart supporters at bargain prices.

At Nicholson's Inn a month after the election, when pieces of the Liberal Party were still hitting the ground, Rod Stewart recounted nomination night to me. He won the nomination by a close vote, 143–131 over Mr. Shaver. However, his victory began to hollow out when, right in the middle of his acceptance speech, Carman Thornton rose from the centre of the crowd of 600 in Tassie Hall and shouted, "That's a pack of lies!" Stewart said he was so unnerved that he could scarcely remember the remainder of his speech, which consisted of all the reasons he had returned to the Liberals.

After some scattered applause, Stewart descended to the convention floor to shake hands with party stalwarts Arthur White, Keith Davey, Eric Strathdee, and Mrs. W. Sheldon, an affable lady who had applauded his every word. Things seemed to be smoothing over until Carman Thornton charged out of the crowd and, his bugging eyes almost touching Stewart's, yelled, "You're a rotten liar!"

Unaware that Mrs. Sheldon at his side had downed a few aperitifs backstage and was emitting inordinate clouds of alcohol fumes, Stewart attributed the smell to Thornton and shouted back, "And you're drunk!"

Mortally insulted, Thornton swung a fist past Stewart's nose. Just as he launched a second swing, several men, including Keith Davey, lifted him off the floor and held him shaking in the air.

Chief Ontario Liberal organizer Eric Strathdee, shaking himself, pushed Stewart out of Tassie Hall and into the school corridor. Stewart said he was shaking, too. Everyone was shaking. Stewart stood on the corridor steps and wondered how he could be hiding alone five minutes after winning the Liberal nomination. But he wasn't alone for long. The hall door burst open, and Carman Thornton charged straight for him.

It flashed through Rod's mind that having a fistfight with the elderly chairman of his own nominating committee wouldn't enhance his chances of being elected. He looked frantically for help, but no one else was there. The two stood nose to nose, and Thornton again waggled his finger. Stewart braced for a fist to land. But, no, Thornton

134

huffed up, looked him in the eye, and hollered, "You smelled Mrs. Sheldon!" And walked away.

The Liberal campaign collapsed right there on the steps. Max Saltsman, in a close race with Jim Chaplin, the Tory candidate, won the election for the NDP that Stewart had defected from. Stewart lost his deposit. Disillusioned, he abandoned politics but went on to write a notable biography of Dr. Norman Bethune. Carman Thornton lived on with his integrity. Eric Strathdee got drunk and shot himself. Keith Davey, the Rainmaker, went on to become a senator. The local Liberals hibernated for twenty-nine years.

63

The Indestructible Unsafe Bridge

The demolition of the Concession Street Bridge in Galt was a crowd pleaser, but it was a disaster for the company hired to blow it up. Back in the 1970s a rumour born in the beverage room of the Overland Hotel intimated that the Concession Street Bridge, one block away, wasn't safe, that it shook when trucks drove across, and that some of the heavier trucks avoided the bridge altogether. Hotel patrons, on their way home, began to tiptoe across.

The bridge had been hammered by ice floes and increasingly heavy traffic since it was built in 1935. How could it not collapse? Politicians and construction companies embraced the rumour, and plans for a new bridge were drawn up. Work was to start in 1976. The new bridge would be four lanes wide, the first two rushed to completion beside the old bridge before it fell of its own weight and the second two laid on the site of the old span as soon as it was removed. And it was decided that the quickest and safest way to remove the old bridge was to blow it up.

Blasting had by then evolved into an art form. Skyscrapers, smokestacks, silos, and old beverage rooms were being dropped on their foundations by skilfully placed charges that blew in sequence like a piano concerto. The Concession Street Bridge was considered a piece of cake. Controlled Blasting of Breslau toiled fourteen hours a day for four days stringing the bridge with 700 pounds of explosive charges as if they were Christmas decorations. The blast was scheduled for noon, August 30, 1977, and most of the kids in town turned out to fantasize that it was their school going up. The police had their usual fits trying to keep the crowd and media out of danger. Only fools, the police told the media, would risk their lives to watch this spectacle.

I hid behind the south end of Leo the Lion's Factory Outlet. Rainer Leipscher, intrepid *Reporter* photographer, stood directly above me on the roof, fully exposed to the blast. By now we were fondly referring to the bridge as the "Old Girl," and we waited with mixed feelings of excitement and wistfulness to see her vaporized. As the moment approached, workmen wearing hard hats walked briskly off the bridge. Then a police siren gave one long wail followed by an eerie silence, like that at the cenotaph as the eleventh hour descended.

The blast exceeded anything we expected. It was a deafening salvo. Jagged chunks of masonry cartwheeled into the river downstream as the bridge disappeared in a dense cloud of smoke and dust. The cloud took the longest time to disperse, but when it did, there was the bridge looking pretty much as it had before. Only one pier at the east end had settled a few feet. People began to cheer.

Up at the blast site demolition experts squinted at blueprints and scratched their hard hats. Pigeons, blasted from their nests, shivered on the ground in shock. Now that the concrete sheathing the bridge had fallen and the girders were laid bare, it became evident why the Old Girl was still standing. It was like peeking up her skirt and seeing iron pants. Steel I beams ran shoulder to shoulder from shore to shore. The bridge had more steel in it per square foot than the bombproof submarine pens at Brest in France.

The Old Girl became an instant legend, a hero to old-timers and a lesson to children concerning strength and integrity and what they could make of their lives if they should ever turn into concrete. The old bridge cost $49,000 to build. The blast cost $30,000 plus the expense of weeks of hammering with the wrecker's ball. It would be interesting to know where all the steel from the old bridge went.

Probably to support several new bridges around the country. The new bridge lanes erected beside the old ones suffered some damage, but at least they didn't fall. I'm told, though, that the new lanes shake a lot when trucks drive across.

64

A Disaster for the Orange Lodge

Cheese Factory Road once crossed Moffat's Creek on a narrow concrete bridge on the sides of which prophets scrawled dooms-day warnings in white paint. Beside the bridge a gravel lane ran through the stream so that you could drive in and wash your car or water your horse. A few yards upstream, in a tree-shaded pool, boys and girls skinny-dipped and compared their anatomical differences. Today the pool is shaded by a towering apartment building.

McBain's apple orchard spread out behind the swimming hole. Next to it was the barn where Grenfell Davenport hid out from his mother and we crawled through the weeds to feed him sandwiches. In front of the barn, on the promontory now overlooking the junction of Cheese Factory Road and Champlain Boulevard, sat the McBain mansion surrounded by pines and cedars. You could drive up to it only through a curving tunnel of cedars. A scary place.

In the 1940s the Hillmers, descendants of the McBains, lived there. Mrs. Hillmer was a staunch supporter of the Orange Lodge. Her only daughter, curiously, became a nun in California. So when Mrs. Hillmer died she left the house and 140 acres to Guy Hillmer, her only son.

I got to see the inside of the house after Guy moved in with his wife and small son. Chancing by when their moving van arrived from British Columbia, I helped them unpack. The house had fourteen Victorian rooms with twelve-foot ceilings, bay windows upstairs and down, and a graceful curving staircase with silk-smooth cherrywood railings and sim-ulated marble steps.

But there was an eerie feeling there. Not good memories. Within two years the Hillmers abandoned the house and moved to Toronto. Later vandals burned it down. Before he left, however, Guy Hillmer, an enlightened and unprejudiced man, sold several acres to the Catholic diocese for the site of Our Lady of Fatima Church honouring a vision of the Virgin Mary seen weeping in the skies over Portugal. So if in passing by the church someday you look up into the sky and see a lady weeping, don't jump to the conclusion that it's the Virgin Mary. It might be Guy Hillmer's mother.

65

Great Moments in Medicine

No book of any sort is complete without a medical section. A few years back a pharmaceutical company published a calendar illustrated each month by what were called "Great Moments in Medicine." The painting for January depicted Louis Pasteur squinting at a test tube held at arm's length over his head. February showed Dr. Frederick Banting doing the same thing with a hypodermic needle. Uplifting but boring.

Why not revive the Great Moments in Medicine calendar but replace the canonized events with some of the lesser known but nonetheless spectacular medical advances born of necessity and ingenuity in our hospital emergency wards? I'm thinking now of the exploits of Dr. John Moffat of Cambridge in the emergency ward of St. Michael's Hospital in Toronto when he was interning there back in the 1950s. I was attending Ryerson Institute at the time and rode home on the train with Dr. Moffat on Friday evenings. Not a trip passed that he didn't recount a gripping medical episode, some of which defied belief. A particularly memorable episode involved a man carried into St. Michael's emergency ward from a nearby Jarvis Street beverage room with a beer glass stuck up his rectum. His pants were awry, and needless to say he was in a squatting position.

Young Dr. Moffat, after examining the man and confirming there was indeed a beer glass rectally secured, decided to call his long-suffering senior doctor for advice. It was after midnight, and one can only imagine the tone of the senior doctor's voice when he was awakened. "What now?"

"Sir," said Dr. Moffat, "we have a patient here with a beer glass secure in his rectum. No, sir, I wouldn't joke with you at this time of night. It's one of those 10 cent draft glasses, narrow at the bottom and globular at the top, shaped like a suppository so that it won't come out. The sphincter muscles are hanging on for dear life. We're afraid of breakage. No, sir, it wasn't served to him that way. I don't know the whole story yet."

Envision the senior doctor squinting into the phone like Louis Pasteur. That itself would make a great January calendar illustration.

"Rough up the interior of the glass with a surgical emery wheel," the senior doctor said. "Then fill the glass with fast-drying plaster of Paris, sink a hook in it, and blow on it until it dries. You don't have to be told what to do next. Lots of luck."

This was done. All the while the man squatted face down on the examining table with his rear aimed at the ceiling like a howitzer. Waiting for the plaster to dry — it took only about fifteen minutes with everyone passing by blowing on it — Dr. Moffat talked to the man. "You're not obliged to tell me how this happened," he said, "but you must understand that I'm curious."

"Well," the man said, "sometimes when the boys in the beer parlour have had a few they do some funny things. Tonight somebody bet that one of us couldn't stick a beer glass up his ass and somehow I got picked to demonstrate. Four men lowered me onto an inverted glass on the table and here I am. I couldn't walk here, but they were good enough to carry me down."

By now the plaster had firmed up and the Great Moment in Medicine was set to occur. After injecting lubricating oil down the sides of the glass, Dr. Moffat, with a flourish, yanked on the hook. The glass, with a pop like a champagne cork, flew out to cheers that could be heard right back at the beer parlour.

Surely, this moment would make a more interesting calendar illustration than Louis Pasteur squinting at his test tube, or a latter-day doctor using a laser to cure snoring.

66

The Viagra Moment

Now on to what is arguably the Greatest Ever Moment in Medicine, at least according to the boys down at the Legion Hall — the discovery of Viagra.

Way back in the twentieth-century, chemists at Pfizer Incorporated tried to formulate a heart pill out of sildenafil citrate. If this medication had been even moderately successful on 40 percent of patients with no more than the usual side effects of delirium, convulsions, tardive dyskinesia, and total loss of bladder control, doctors would now be prescribing it for a modest $2 or $3 a pill, which would earn the company an exorbitant profit over and above the customary class-action lawsuits. Unfortunately, the medication tended to stop hearts and had an alarming side effect of giving male patients erections. Credit Pfizer's promotion department into turning a costly defeat into a Great Moment in Medicine and marketing Viagra for $15 a pill.

Although months passed before our food and drug administration approved Viagra for sale in Canada, its effects here were immediate. Service club bus trips to Buffalo quadrupled, the sale of lottery tickets dropped, and on some days no one turned up in the Senate at all. Viagra, according to my tax-deductible pharmaceutical receipts, finally went on sale here April 11, 2000.

To match this Great Moment in Medicine for men, Energy Brands Incorporated of Whitestone, New York, produced what it claimed was a carbonated aphrodisiac and called it "Viagra for women." This patented brand name couldn't be used, of course, so the company called its product Go-Go Passion. It came in 8.4-fluid-ounce disposable environmentally friendly pop cans and contained 150 milligrams of Siberian ginseng, twenty milligrams of yohimbe (prescribed before Viagra for male erectile dysfunction and other euphemisms), and twenty milligrams of zinc, which is also good for tinnitus in your ears. As soon as Go-Go Passion was approved for sale in Britain, the Roman Catholic Church of Scotland became outraged. Although it approved of more babies, it didn't want them conceived on the dance floor.

Back in Canada the ever-vigilant Royal Canadian Legion, monitoring these sexual insurgencies outflanking the vets who didn't want to be left stranded on the beach again, added to its appeal for more modern weapons for our armed forces free Viagra for service survivors of all wars. User-friendly Viagra was a welcome technical improvement over the old vacuum tumescent devices with their backpacks, air tanks, and dangling hose connections, which always aroused the ladies' suspicions at Legion dances. Veterans Affairs Canada in Ottawa received up to 1,000 requests a month for the pill which, at $15 a shot, was equal to the price of a mortar shell and left gaping craters in veterans' service pensions.

Government approval was finally given so that Canadian veterans of both world wars and lesser events such as the Korean and both Gulf wars became eligible for up to six free Viagra pills per month, barring a class-action suit by the ladies' auxiliary. Conservative MP Elsie Wayne called the Viagra for veterans plan a total waste of $1.5 million a year, virtually assuring herself a crushing defeat at the next federal election.

Since the average age of World War II veterans is now eighty-two, it appears that veterans of more recent wars have benefited the most. But don't count out the older warhorses. If they can make it to the cenotaph, they can make it to the bedroom, even if it requires the assistance of home care.

Which brings to mind the story of the ninety-year-old veteran who went to a priest to confess he had committed adultery. The priest told the man that although he had indeed committed a cardinal sin, it was a remarkable feat and how had it come about? The old man said it was accomplished under a kitchen table at the Orange Lodge. The priest, shocked, wanted to know what a good Catholic was doing at the Orange Lodge, and the man said he wasn't a Catholic but a loyal Orangeman. The priest, shocked all the more, then wanted to know what a loyal Orangeman was doing in a Catholic confessional booth.

"Father," the old veteran said, "when you're ninety years old and you commit adultery you tell everybody."

67
The G Spot Unleashed

*N*ow that Viagra has made a lot of us old goats dangerous again, the ladies are making the best of it by reactivating their G spot which, I gather from scarcely intelligible and disgusting medical literature, is a bean-shaped erogenous zone that lurks in their private parts and is capable of unleashing orgasms powerful enough to hurl an elderly man right out the bedroom window.

The G in the spot is named after its discoverer, the German gynecologist Ernst Gräfenberg, not to be confused with the *Hindenburg*, which blew up at Lakehurst, New Jersey, in 1937. Actually, the Gräfenberg spot has been around since creation (Queen Victoria is alleged to have used it extensively) but fell into disuse after Sigmund Freud insisted on stimulating another spot. Gräfenberg rediscovered it when he accidentally stepped on his wife in 1940.

I find this too embarrassing to go on, but if you suspect I'm making it all up, just nip over to the nearest bookstore and buy *The G Spot*, a *New York Times* bestseller available for $8.99 as a Dell paperback. The hardcover edition costs five times as much but comes with a whiplash collar.

68
The Prostate — A Piece of Cake

I, make a point of not whining and snivelling about my personal ordeals, but this one is too good to miss. One day in November 2002 I turned off the radio in the middle of an election commercial, ran out of the house, hopped into my car, and drove off through the misty autumn countryside to Guelph to have a biopsy on my prostate gland. I plan to check my prostate, or what's left of it, as a diversion from every election from now on. The ladies, cheated at creation from having this diversionary gland, will just have to settle for a mammogram.

The biopsy wasn't in my original plans. I intended to have just a PSA (prostate specific antigen) test. I first heard about the PSA test from Verne Cavanaugh, a good friend in Brantford who shares my aversion to having doctors ram their fat fingers up the rectum in the traditional digital test. These digits are different from the ones used in computers and movie soundtracks. So beware. Verne said that a PSA involved a simple blood test. There would be no dropping of the trousers, and I would only have to roll up one sleeve — at last a prostate test with dignity! Since all men over fifty are urged to have their prostates tested annually and I was twenty years overdue, I arranged to have a test pronto. And it was, as Verne said, a piece of cake.

A healthy prostate is supposed to have a PSA rating of four. Mine came back seven. Dr. Achiume said there was no cause for alarm, that ten was considered the danger level, but to be safe he would refer me to a urologist for another look. Urologists in Cambridge being scarce and the waiting list lengthy, he referred me to Dr. Gordon Thompson in Guelph, genial and reassuring with a keen interest in hockey, but with fingers the size of corncobs.

"I hope you don't mind the old digital test," he said. That done he said he couldn't find anything disturbing, but just to be safe referred me to the hospital across the street, St. Joseph's, for a transrectal ultrasound and biopsy. Just another look. A piece of cake, he told me.

There are complications with these tests. No blood-thinning aspirin for ten days prior to the tests, but antibiotics two days before and after. While on the antibiotics I had to avoid eating zinc, iron, sucralfate, magnesium, calcium, and aluminum, all the things I loved. In addition, on my own cognizance, I avoided pregnant women. I was warned that the antibiotics might cause nausea, dizziness, headaches, diarrhea, tendonitis, changes in vision, restlessness, ringing in the ears, and mental disturbances. *Me* with mental disturbances! I was also cautioned to wear protective outdoor clothing because the drugs would make me sensitive to sunlight. Indeed, sunscreen was in order. I won't list all the interactions this antibiotic has with a long list of other drugs, including alcohol and caffeine, because it would sound too much like an election platform. To top it all (or bottom it) I had to give myself a Fleet enema one hour before the ultrasound test.

The transrectal ultrasound test, you'll be glad to know, Verne, was indeed a piece of cake (chocolate) because it was administered by two lovely young ladies. It involved shoving a camera (not a Pentax or Speed Graphic, but a miniaturized marvel in a lubricated tube half the diameter of one of Dr. Thompson's fingers) up my rectum to photograph the prostate close up. The girls said I wasn't the first patient to mention the size of Dr. Thompson's fingers. The girls were chatty, and we had a lot of laughs. I told them I would love a close-up of my prostate to send to my good friend Verne Cavanaugh on a Christmas card. As soon as the girls were finished, a male doctor whose name escapes me, came in to perform the biopsy, which involved guiding a needle up the ultrasound transducer into the prostate. Another piece of cake.

"When I count to three," the doctor said, "don't move! Because that's when I pull the trigger on the gun."

The gun!" I cried. "Nobody told me about the gun."

"Don't worry," he said. "I'm not firing anything into you. I'm snipping a little bit out. One, two, three ..."

Bang! I felt a little bee sting way up inside.

"There," he said. "Most men don't really mind this at all. Just five more shots."

"Five more shots," I said. "They don't use that many in a firing squad." I was a barrel of laughs.

Before I could go home I had to sit, sulking, on a pad until the bleeding stopped. I wanted to strangle Verne. I had to wait another two weeks for the test results. One disturbing side effect of the tests was that I developed a compulsion to spin about while walking whenever I imagined footsteps behind me and, if passing a wall, to edge sideways with my back to it. I was told this was a normal reaction that would wear off months before the next prostate test or election, whichever came first.

144

69

Damn!

*A*fter all those "make-sures" to confirm I didn't have *it*, I learned I had indeed gotten it. Prostate cancer.

Let's skim over the treatment — the hormone shots, months of waiting for the CT scans, the trial run and target tattooing, the seven weeks of radiation at Henderson Hospital in Hamilton, the thirty-five round trips down from Glen Morris, and the stops to pee on the way home.

Doctors insist that men undergo radiation with full bladders in order to better aim the neutron accelerator, and every time I went to the treatment room, quaffing one last slug from my water bottle, I was passed at the door by the previous patient sprinting for the lavatory. Incontinence threatened for several hours afterwards, and I had two pit stops on the way home, one behind a fat oak tree on Mineral Springs Road and another under the Canadian National Railways overpass on Highway 99, the main reason I preferred to drive my self down and back.

I had to learn how to kegel, an exercise designed to strengthen the muscles that control the bladder. Pregnant women know what I am talking about. To kegel one must contract one's sphincter muscles until, as a prominent urologist suggests, one's buttocks can hold a $10 bill on a windy hill. To be truly capable of bladder control, he suggests you hold a $50 bill in your buttocks on a windy hill, but not in a full-blown gale.

After the treatment, I had to return to Henderson for periodic assessment, part of which was a quiz to monitor my *through-put*, a term usually applied to oil pipeline flow. Usually, a lady doctor did the quiz and always left me with the impression that she neither heard my answers nor cared.

"How's your stream, Mr. Green? Is it reliable? Is it strong during the day?"

"Five minutes ago it was almost uncontrollable."

"Uh-huh." Scribble, scribble. "How many glasses of water do you drink each day?"

"Eight, sometimes ten."

"Uh-huh. And how many times do you get up during the night?"

"Eight, sometimes ten."

"Uh-huh. How strong is your stream at night?"

"I'm thinking about joining a volunteer fire department."

"Good, Mr. Green. Everything sounds right on course. Dr. Sathya will be with you in a minute. Just hang your pants over the chair."

Dr. Sathya entered, holding the questionnaire the lady doctor had just handed him. "Uh-huh, I see everything looks right on course. Now since you've removed your pants, I might as well give you the old digital test. It's overdue. Bend over the chair." A few moments later Dr. Sathya handed me a fresh prescription for stool softeners and said, "See you in six months. Drink lots of water at bedtime and get as much unbroken sleep as possible. And, above all, don't worry about the cancer. Something else will get you first. You could even be run over by a truck on your way from here to the parking garage."

Each time I go down for a checkup I notice something I hadn't noticed before. The last time I observed that a very high proportion of men in the prostate treatment line wear hearing aids. I think it might be connected to rectal examinations. I can't hear a damn thing for ten minutes after mine. Also, I get backaches from walking on my toes.

70

The Geezer Squeezer

Here's another Great Moment in Medicine we shouldn't pass up, brought about not by medical researchers but by two seventy-six-year-old retired mechanical engineers, both prostate cancer survivors.

Incontinence, as it's known by the medical fraternity, and which prostate cancer survivors call "leaking," is a common aftereffect of prostate cancer treatment, more so for the surgery than for radiation. Doctors in the United States alone create an estimated 40,000 leakers a year. Imagine what that does to the water table.

The medical establishment offers little relief from leakage except adult diapers and more surgery. So Chuck Single and Jack Cochrane of the Ann Arbor, Michigan, prostate cancer support group decided to solve the problem right at the faucet, so to speak. Mr. Single, the leaker of the two, created the prototype device, and Mr. Cochrane, who doesn't leak, helped refine it by working on Mr. Single.

They concocted (there's a pun for you) a simple clamp comprised of stainless steel and foam padding that a man can affix to his euphemism and shut off the flow of urine without interrupting the blood supply. They call it the Geezer Squeezer and have patented it. It can be worn, they claim, without discomfort for up to eighteen hours, long enough to drive from Galt to Hespeler and back when there is a train blocking Highway 24, though it's advisable to release the device every few hours for palliative relief.

So there you have it, leakers. Unhook yourselves from your windshield washer tanks, turn on the Internet, and visit website *GeezerSqueezer.com* for full details. But be prepared to explain to U.S. Customs that the squeezer isn't a detonating device. The deluxe Geezer Squeezer comes with a "full" sign semaphore that pops up from under the shirt collar and is activated by a hearing-aid battery if it's part of the Phonak digital system.

71
Tiddly, Anyone?

*A*nd before we leave geezers. When I first worked on the *Galt Reporter* in 1956, I was handed a list of words prohibited in a decent family newspaper. One of those words was *television*. Another was *penis*. The *Reporter* has long since accepted *television* as a nonthreatening word, but not until the sensational and unavoidable Lorena Bobbitt trial in the United States did the paper reluctantly spell out *penis*. If this trial of the woman who cut off her husband John's penis had occurred in 1956, I can't imagine the euphemisms the *Reporter* would have resorted to. *Tiddly* springs to mind. My mother and all my aunts, except Auntie Bea, were well aware of what a penis was, but they would never utter the word. They called it a tiddly.

Whenever, as a boy, I went to Auntie Lou's house to walk her dog, Sport, in the winter, she would say, "Now don't stay out in the cold until you freeze your tiddly." Then she would fall into maniacal laughter for perhaps five minutes. There was a game called Tiddly Winks that I was too embarrassed to play. Until I was thirteen I thought a penis was someone who played the piano, a misconception prolonged by a couple of piano players I knew who fitted the description quite well.

Anyway, *tiddly* went out the window with John Bobbitt's penis. Family newspapers everywhere abandoned prudery and slapped *penis* all over their front pages along with graphic accounts of amputations and mutilations around the world. In Toronto a prominent eye surgeon's penis was attacked by his wife snapping a pair of pinking scissors. A man in Pittsburgh was shortened by an electric roast carver. And poor Chou En Quang in Singapore, after a spat with his wife, rushed to his third-storey window in time to see his penis being carried off by a dog ("Here boy, here boy!").

Before Lorena Bobbitt's trial a militant U.S. feminist group declared that if she were convicted they would castrate 100 men. And there's another word we couldn't use in 1956 — *castrate*. Little wonder the streets filled with men who appeared to have been stricken overnight by osteoporosis and walked in a defensive crouch. I spotted a quarter on the curb one day by walking that way.

Hysteria reached the stage where men were advised to have their names tattooed on their penis in case the police retrieved it from a ditch and tossed it into a box with half a dozen others picked up that night. This was all very well if you had a short name, but what about all the Swartzentrubers and McGillicuttys? Also having your name tattooed on your penis was no guarantee of ownership at the lost-and-found. The pace at emergency wards was hectic and mistakes occurred.

Imagine if you had a name like (to pick one out of the hat) "Bob" and you woke up on the operating table to discover your penis had "Leonard" on it. Malpractice suits would spring to mind, even though Leonard was longer.

I still prefer *tiddly*, or at my age maybe *geezer*.

72
Worst of All — M.S.UR.ATION

$\mathcal{M}$uch of the *Cambridge Reporter's* charm was that it respected the primness of a small town, unlike the insensitive abandon of big-city papers in their zeal to tell it as it is. The *Reporter* drew the line.

For instance, our mother paper, the *Toronto Star*, once ran in its Friday health section an article by Judy Gerstal on the benefits of masturbation. Try to imagine MASTURBATION in a four-column headline. A few years ago Clyde Warrington, when he was a most discreet editor on the *Reporter*, used this same term in a lower type case and a three-column headline and was very nearly fired. Shocked readers phoned in to remind him that his paper was distributed in Glen Morris.

So I wouldn't dare mention the word again if it weren't involved in yet another great medical breakthrough. *The British Journal of Urology International* claims (and here I revert to the dot-dot code of the *Reporter*) that mas...b.tion is essential to good physical and mental health and can actually prevent prostate cancer. Now they tell me. When I was a boy, Lord Baden-Powell, founder of the Boy Scouts, claimed that the beastly practice "drove men insane and made boys go blind." I quit when I had to wear glasses and now I have prostate cancer.

Australian researchers, whose articles appear in the British urology journal, say that semen is potent and brews chemicals that turn carcinogenic if left lying around. "The more you flush out the ducts," they say, "the less semen there is to fester." And they urge all males aged twenty to fifty to m..tur..te at least six days a week. Which still leaves Sunday open for prayer.

The spoiler in this great revelation, according to researcher Graham Giles, is that lots of normal sex with the ladies is not as beneficial as m.st.rb.tion, that infections acquired from normal sex might actually increase the risk of prostate cancer. Another caution. Men wearing whiplash collars are probably overdoing it and should take up drumming.

And what do the ladies get out of all this? Perturbation, perfectly proper to spell out in a four-column headline until someone discovers that it can make them go blind.

73
Almost As Bad —
M.D.I.C.T.ON

*L*et's consider the medications we lavish on our faltering organs and the growing menace of drug side effects or collateral damage, as the military would say. Now that scientists have revealed that female hormone replacement therapy (enhanced pregnant mares' urine) causes what scientists for decades claimed it prevented — heart failure, strokes, cancer, et cetera — a lot of ladies have pitched their pills and gone back to hot flushes and ill temper, kicking their doctors in their groins and loudly accusing perfectly strange men on the street with having erectile dysfunction. But not to worry. It's to our good health to learn that everything doctors prescribe for us causes what it's supposed to prevent — and often worse.

Take Valium, for example, a tranquilizer commonly prescribed for nervous menopausal women and anthropologists with stress incontinence. It's supposed to calm you down, but if you read the side effects, you'll discover that it causes anxiety, fatigue, depression, acute hyper-excited states, hallucinations, and muscle spasms. Also, it's addictive.

I quit taking Celebrex for my arthritis when I read that the side effects can include hives, vomiting, fatigue, swelling of the feet, mental confusion, depression, and hearing problems. The Lovastatin I take to lower my blood cholesterol makes me liable for muscle cramps, uncommon fatigue, blurred vision, headaches, heartburn or stomach pain, persistent skin rash and, according to Dr. Gifford Jones, a detectable tendency towards suicide and homicide. I gave up taking Flomax (increases urine flow) for my prostate when I found it made me dizzy and unable to sleep and (confirmed in print by the manufacturer) gave me a runny nose.

The answer to this expensive and contradictory alchemy? Religion for one. But it can cause severe weight loss in your wallet.

Take cynical satisfaction in learning that the pharmaceutical companies cranking out antidepressant pills to take our minds off the side effects of all our other medications are in need of antidepressant medications themselves for relief of increasing legal side effects. The U.S. Food and Drug Administration is threatening to restrict and fine SmithKline Beecham, maker of the antidepressant Paxil, for making false and misleading claims. The Upjohn Company has been caught bribing pharmacists to persuade doctors to switch to their drugs. So what sort of antidepressants do pharmaceutical companies take? Lawyers. Hard to swallow but tax deductible. So is promotion, even if it's misleading, because the lawyers have contrived to have it classed as "research."

It's worth noting that the latest round of antidepressants were developed from mixing various chemicals with ground-up rat brains and running them through a centrifuge to find what are called "serotonin reuptake blockers." As one pharmacist said, "It has taken a million bloody rat brains to make us happy." One ground-up lawyer's brain would make some people happy. And how are psychiatrists coping with the rising suicide rate? They are contributing to it by having the highest suicide rate of all the professions. Dentists are second, dental patients third and, believe it or not, schoolteachers have the lowest rate. Nurses have a low rate, too, but mainly because their hands shake too much to shoot straight.

Perhaps we should reconsider some of the discarded medical treatments of the 1920s — quaint but comforting. I turn now to Bernarr Macfadden's magazine *Physical Culture*, loaned to me by Don Renwick of Ayr, Ontario. Macfadden was the great health guru of the 1920s and 1930s whose advice was followed and trusted by the grandmothers of today's pharmaceutical lawyers. The edition I have is dated April 1928, so one must concede that some of his medical truths have been amended, but not much.

Macfadden's "washout routine" is credited with curing most illnesses in addition to preventing cancer: "Rapidly drink six tall glasses of hot water and follow up with vigorous exercise." The vigorous exercise isn't optional; it's unavoidable. Doctors today urge us to drink eight tall glasses of water per day but not necessarily hot or all at once. Progress. Macfadden was a keen proponent of colonic irrigation, which is too embarrassing to discuss here, even though it's still in vogue right here in Cambridge, too. You won't find the practitioners listed in the Yellow Pages, but they can readily be tracked down in the Grand River Healing Waters Directory available free at most local health-food stores.

Princess Diana was a big fan of colonic irrigation and spoke highly of the "banquet treatment." Don't let your imagination dwell on that very long. Colonic treatment advertisements flood Macfadden's magazine. Tyrrell's Hygienic Institute claims that "a dead colon is what ails eight out of ten people today" and extols the glorious relief afforded by its Cascade Machine. Two out of ten people did, however, have other worries, and Macfadden directs them to his learned colleagues.

David V. Bush promises in his book *Spunk* to give you "Bull Dog Courage" in forty-eight hours or your money back — 50 cents — if you have the nerve to ask for it. For a mere 10 cents B.N. Bogue will stop you from stammering. Dr. Benedict Lust will put you in perfect condition for life for $1. The Perfect Breather Company promotes a head harness that will stop you from snoring. And noses are reshaped with the Anita Nose Adjuster for women and the Trilety Trados nose shaper for men, which was awarded a medal for excellence at the Wembley Exposition in England.

In a medical advice column a girl writes: "The skin of my lower body has broken out in pimples. I am also having to urinate at night. I am only sixteen, and these conditions worry me a great deal."

Macfadden advises her to "avoid candies and all sweet stuff and all sexual excitement. Also, breathe deeply and drink more water."

In those reliable days even cookbooks carried extensive medical advice. Rosemary Ferguson loaned me the fiftieth edition of the *Home Cookbook* compiled by the ladies of Toronto and chief cities and towns across Canada. The fiftieth edition came out in 1877.

Consider Mrs. Gardiner's fig paste remedy for constipation: "one half pound of good figs chopped fine, one half pint of molasses, two ounces powdered senna leaves, and one dram of fine powdered cardamom seed. Boil molasses, then stir in all the rest and boil again. A teaspoonful once in a while is a dose (stand well back). It will, when covered, keep for a year." Mrs. Gardiner doesn't say how to cover the patient. She adds that to restore a person struck by lightning, "shower with cold water for two hours. If patient shows no sign of life, add salt to the water and shower for an hour longer."

After that, I guess, you start digging. Lightning today is cited as an excellent cure for constipation, not to mention earwax, but it's difficult to schedule and isn't covered by Medicare. The cure for boils, according to Mrs. Gardiner, is Isaiah 27:21.

74

Alternative Medicine's Effect on World War II

As we try to assess the impact of alternative medicine on the twentieth century, our considerations turn unavoidably to Adolf Hitler and his blind faith in Dr. Theodor Morell. Albert Speer, Hitler's minister of armaments and war production, referred to Dr. Morell as "a screwball," but Morell's unorthodox medicine appealed to Hitler's mystical mind, and he kept him by his side until the bitter end.

Hitler had long been plagued with gastrointestinal disturbances and fretted because he had to interrupt important meetings because of gas pains. A hypochondriac and a vegetarian, he avoided orthodox doctors for fear they might recommend he eat a sausage.

Dr. Morell was just the ticket. He determined that Hitler's problems resulted from "a complete exhaustion of his intestinal flora" and prescribed capsules of "Multiflor" washed down by Fachinger mineral water. This procedure was followed up with injections of biologicals extracted from bulls' testicles "from the best livestock of a Bulgarian peasant." I am not making this up but am quoting Speer in his autobiography *Inside the Third Reich*. Speer was, at times, the number two man in Hitler's top echelon. Good initial results impressed the Führer so that he urged all his friends to consult Morell. The doctor examined Eva Braun, but she described him as "disgustingly dirty" and vowed never to let him touch her again.

Hermann Göring's alternative medicine consisted of a shot of morphine (to which he became addicted during treatment for his injuries after his fighter plane was shot down in World War I) and a few hours with his enormous model train layout, which he kept in his attic. Rudolf Hess patronized an alternative medicine doctor of his own liking who prescribed for him a vegetarian diet quite different from Hitler's. He frequently sneaked a bag of the prescribed food into Hitler's luncheons until one day, according to Speer, the Führer found out and ordered Hess to eat at home. This unpleasantness, combined with Hitler's foul breath, was probably the real reason the moody Hess flew to England in 1941.

Once Morell got Hitler's bowels functioning properly, the inevitable happened — flatulence. The Führer wasn't amused, believing it didn't befit a man of his almost divine stature to cough in his trousers. Morell to the rescue again. He fed Hitler large quantities of Dr. Koester's (another screwball) anti-gas pills compounded of belladonna and strychnine. These, according to Alan Bullock in his biography of Hitler, accounted for the dictator's ash-grey pallor and shaking limbs near the end of his life.

New evidence served up by Professor Michel Perrier of the University of Lausanne indicates that not only was Hitler hounded by flatulence but that he also had severe periodontal gum disease that gave him halitosis worse than that of Canada's wartime prime minister, William Lyon Mackenzie King. Computer-enhanced images of Hitler's teeth from film footage of some of his more uninhibited speeches reveal tooth decay, abscesses, and gum disease, Perrier claims. This contention agrees with evidence given to Americans in 1945 by Hitler's dentist, U.S.-trained Dr. Hugo Blaschke, and five X-rays of Hitler's head that turned up in a Washington, D.C., archive.

I believe you can also find these X-rays at Pete's Fine Junk on Ainslie Street in Galt.

Hitler rejected all of Blaschke's suggestions about replacing the rotten teeth with dentures, for fear they might fly out during an impassioned speech at Nuremberg and ricochet off the lectern in full view of Pathé newsreel cameras. So there we have it. The gas turned off at one end and foul breath at the other. Not a barrel of laughs. During his final years, Hitler forced Morell's medications onto most of the members of his entourage, and their consequent noxious mental state, like his, made for a much less pleasant war than would have otherwise occurred.

Benito Mussolini, on the other hand, brushed his teeth and passed gas with abandon. "Fartus Stupendous," he was called in Rome. This liberal attitude inspired his son, Romano Mussolini, to become a world-renowned jazz piano player. (He played a concert at Mohawk College in Hamilton in 1994.) And Benito's unbridled behaviour wasn't lost on his army which, even if it meant surrendering, loved to play soccer with the enemy and showed a marked aversion to violence.

I didn't intend to put down alternative medicine — just give a cautionary lesson from history. In hindsight Hitler would probably now say, "All things in moderation."

And before we leave flatulence, this item about Dr. Colin Leaky (his real name), a serious researcher in Cambridge, England. He's invented a device that accurately measures the components of flatulence. He calls it a "flatometer" and claims it's an essential tool in establishing how much human emissions are thinning out the ozone layer. As the population grows, he says, so grows the cloud of flatulent methane and carbon dioxide that's destroying our protective ozone. By the time we have seven billion people aboard the planet, we'll have to apply sunscreen just to make it from the house to the car. Dr. Leaky, who owns a micro-research company called Peas and Beans, hopes to develop a diet low in ozone-depleting gases.

Terry Bolin, a gastroenterologist (try saying that with a mouthful of chili), and his research teammate, Rosemary Stanton, a nutritionist, have just completed the first large-scale clinical study of flatulence in Australia, presumably on the Woomera Rocket Range. They have released their findings in a book entitled *Wind Breaks: Coming to Terms with Flatulence.*

75
Maturity It's Called

Thirty years ago I began to discuss with my friends the coming senility, the day when we would start to think and talk like our parents. Len Iseler said that his mother firmly believed that the bushes surrounding her nursing home were swarming with bootleggers. The year before, when she was in Cambridge Memorial Hospital, she was convinced that the golf course next door was swarming with prostitutes disguised as geese. A Catholic lady in the next bed misunderstood and came to believe that the golf course was swarming with Protestants, which was even worse. Iris Mitten's mother, who happened to be in CMH at the same time, but two floors up, had a better view and said that in reality the course was swarming with lawyers, no doubt waiting for doctors facing malpractice suits. Some of these lawyers held flags and didn't leave until it snowed.

While working as a porter at CMH, I saw many relatives and friends enter this other world (and the one close behind). A man who served with my dad in the 111th Battalion in World War I appointed himself warden in the 5A long-term-care ward. One night, during a thunderstorm, he approached me from the river observation lounge and aimed a metal urinal at me like a flashlight. "Don't go near the windows," he said. "There's a lot of incoming stuff."

My Uncle Bill Bate was convinced that the Department of Highways was holding him in the hospital so that he would be forced to miss his eighty-fourth-birthday driver's test. One day my Auntie Bea went to visit him in the intensive-care ward, forgetting that he had been moved up to room 585, and sat with the wrong man for two hours. "How was I to know when he had that mask on?" she asked.

My mother, during her last days, also made it to room 585. There was no view of the golf course from there, so she was free to think of more important things. "When I pass on," she said one day near the end, "your father's going to marry one of those Red Cross homekeepers. Watch her, because she'll lock you in your room."

I was only fifty-seven at the time, so the warning seemed credible. She also said, "When I pass on, get your father into a home or he'll drive you crazy." So we got him into a home, but he drove us crazy, anyway. He had a phone. To complain he couldn't sleep, he phoned George Hees, the federal minister of defence; he phoned the mayor; and he phoned anyone else who came to mind.

Sleep is crucial. Without it we begin to see strange things on the golf course. I can still sleep, and I believe that is what has saved my mind. Mind you, I have to sit with my feet in a bowl of tepid salt water and my head out the window so I can see if anyone is sneaking up on me, but it beats going strange.

76

The Devil's Therapy

I've been involved in music since my teens, and I credit this, along with getting enough sleep, with preventing me from going strange. Music is an accepted therapy. The trouble is one person's musical therapy is another person's nervous breakdown. Jazz, which I love, drives some people to see the devil. *The Pocket Quarterly of Recreation*, published by the Church Recreation Service of Chicago in 1928, warns of the devilish ingredients in jazz and modern dance and quotes some knowledgeable authorities.

A leader of the Young Men's Christian Association claimed that "listening to jazz or playing the terrible music would make devils out of saints." The little blue book goes on to say: "It requires no mental effort to enjoy jazz. A moronic intelligence can absorb all that it has to offer." My parents told me the same thing. "The beat of the tom tom," the book warns, "which drives savages into orgiastic frenzies, and the beat of the jazz drum setting the pace for the modern dance are identical." This phenomenon might explain why Baptists never have sex standing up: they're afraid people will think they're dancing.

A noted preacher of the time, Dr. Joseph Lee, offered the only sensible solution. "The problem with the social dance would be 95 percent solved," he said, "if there was no dancing between members of the opposite sex." How pleased he would be to know that this finally came about in some of our elite clubs.

77

Alternative Therapy — The Bass Drum

lthough the religious right has condemned drums, it has used them extensively to pound grace into the minds of infidels. Mainly, it has relied on the bass drum, God's metronome, playable in all keys at once and sounding up close like a cannon and far away like a heartbeat.

The Salvation Army springs to mind. Now its gentle bass drumbeat sounds like retreating thundershowers, but it wasn't always so. D.A. Smith, in his book *At the Forks of the Grand*, draws from the *Brant Review* and the *Paris Star* riotous drum battles between the Salvation Army and the rival Gospel Army for the souls of Paris in 1884 and 1885.

Major Atherton of the Gospel Army punctuated his services with bass drumbeats, and at one particularly emotional meeting in a park caused a young man to cry out that he was going to die. After the man fell to the ground, the major rushed to his side to kneel and pray for him to rise. This the man did, only to vomit all over the major's head.

The women who powered the Salvation Army pounded around the town, shouting, "God bless the drum! Give it to the drum!" But after causing a town councillor's horse to bolt with its cutter, the pretty and vivacious Captain Nellie Todd was charged and convicted of disturbing the peace. She refused to pay the $2 fine and so was escorted to the jail in Brantford, but allegedly on the way she converted the bailiff. The Paris Salvation Army beat the drum all the way to Galt in a late-nineteenth-century crusade and set Salvationists here to pounding until children cried and horses bolted. The Galt army, however, chose to pay the fine and tone down the drum.

The military has never muted its bass drums, which keep the troops in step even when they're drunk.

78

The Beat Goes On

In 1884, the same year Major Atherton was savaging Paris with his drum, George Steep picked up a forty-five-pound concert bass drum and became the heartbeat of the 29th Regiment of Galt years before the Boer War. He pounded the drum through that war and World War I and then, with the Galt Kiltie Band, right through World War II. Sixty years. When he retired from the Kiltie Band in 1945, he turned his drum over to Neil Harvey, who pounded it until 1947 when its relentless weight threatened to give him curvature of the spine. With a lighter drum Mr. Harvey powered the Kilties until 1985. Two bass drummers — 100 years.

Both George Steep and Neil Harvey have passed on, but the great concert bass drum rests in the Kiltie Band instrument room waiting for a drummer of Steep's super-strength to hoist it and beat it until Judgment Day.

The bass drummer's greatest hazard is that he can't see where he's going. I can still see the bass drummer with the Ayr-Paris Band at the Drumbo Fair parading around the livestock ring with cow flaps the size of pumpkin pies stuck to his feet, his eyes bugging out, pounding his drum as if he were tanning a hide while the rest of the band picked its way through this minefield squeaking out of tune.

Don Elsegood, for many years the bass drummer with the Highland Fusiliers in Galt, related a few scary experiences when the pulse fluttered and the band nearly fell apart. At an opening ceremony for a bonspiel at the Galt Country Club the Fusiliers had to stand at attention on the rink while some notables gave speeches. When at last the band got the order to march, its members, frozen to the ice, had to lean forward forty-five degrees before their boots ripped free. Mr. Elsegood almost went over the top of his bass and came close to beating it with his feet. Skating judges, he said, would have given him a score of 5.9.

On another day, while leading a parade to Victoria Park in Galt, the Fusiliers turned onto the grass and Mr. Elsegood marched hard into a fire hydrant. "Stabbing pain bit into both knees," he said, "and for some reason I thought I was being attacked by wild dogs."

"Get away, you bastards!" he shouted, kicking out both feet high in the air. The rest of the band, thinking he had drunk too much at the armoury, soldiered on down the park while he pirouetted and screamed obscenities. "I didn't miss a beat, though," he said.

Sometimes a Salvation Army bass drum still speaks out. In 1997 an army band was turning a corner at the top of Powell Street on the brink of the steepest hill in San Francisco when the bass drummer twisted his ankle on a cable-car track and fell. His drum broke from its clip and rolled down the hill, accelerating to perhaps forty miles per hour. It missed a cable car by inches and sent pedestrians diving for their lives.

Near the bottom of the hill, at full speed, the drum grazed a car fender, took to the air like a Frisbee, and smashed through the large front window of a gay bar. Inside it cleared off a table of drinks and landed with a boom flat against a wall with its Salvation Army emblem upright. The bartender, Arthur Mellon, said, "Just last week the Unitarians told us God was on our side ... and now this!"

Horn players suffer different disasters. Bill Goddard, a jazz saxophone player, somehow wound up conducting the pit orchestra at the now-defunct Casino on Queen Street in Toronto. One night, he said, a scantily clad lady doing handstands on a white horse manoeuvred too close to the edge of the stage. A hind hoof of her horse probed the air and settled onto a trombone player's bald head, almost pushing it below his collar. He played on, however, but after the horse lifted its hoof he was left with a perfect red imprint of a horseshoe on his pate.

Phil Pratt, after a narrow escape from the beaches of Dunkirk, played out the war in the Army Show in England. Returning to Galt in 1945, he formed a seven-piece band to play at the Masonic Hall on Dickson Street. There was a dance every Saturday night. The Masonic, he said, was more dangerous than Dunkirk. One of his saxophone players, Freddy Legge, had a drinking problem, as did most of the people dancing. But Freddy's was worse. Near the end of a dance, Freddy rolled off his chair and lay on his back with his tenor saxophone clutched to his chest. Pratt let him lie there until it was time for the national anthem. Dance bands then always played "God Save the King" to end the dance and cool the fights. "Get up, Freddy, the King," Pratt said. Freddy didn't move. So after the anthem, Pratt called upon the crowd for "a big hand for Freddy Legge and his horizontal saxophone." Everyone whistled and cheered, but Freddy didn't hear. He had to be carried down the stairs.

Les Kadar, who runs the Garden Gate Lawn and Garden Statuary Centre in the old Nicholson's Inn at Blair, used to play trumpet in a rock band. Playing in a dive in Welland in the 1960s, he and his band accompanied an exotic dancer who loved to pirouette so that her enormous silicon bosom would float like the *Graf Zeppelin*. The stage was too small, and that night one of her breasts lodged in the bell of Les's trumpet, driving it into his mouth and almost knocking out his front teeth. His mouth bled, and she offered to kiss it better but, like a gentleman, he declined and offered first aid for her breasts.

79
Amazing Grace and Other Disasters

There was no escape from exotic dancers.

I had the pleasure of playing drums with what was considered "a class act," a trio fronted by Charlie Rush, a fine Irish tenor whom Alex Barris, a noted Toronto entertainment critic, said was as good as any he had heard in the clubs, and George Alonzo, an accordion player compared with Vic Central, Canada's finest. Charlie Rush also played bass fiddle. We were all from Galt and might have brought home the Order of Canada but for our association with exotic dancers. Club owners wouldn't let us perform without them, so our group, the Chuck Allan Trio, was always billed as accompaniment for Chi Chi O'Connor and her horse Mr. Windybars, Patty Ann "40D Cup" Mayo, Princess Elke, and Kitty Carr.

Princess Elke claimed to have had an affair with Punch Imlach, coach of the Toronto Maple Leafs back in the 1960s when the hockey team won Stanley Cups. She flashed a large diamond ring she said he had given her and showed off photos of him with his arms around her. The princess also had pictures of the team's players with their arms around her and hinted that her name might be on the Stanley Cup.

Kitty Carr didn't make it that far up the social ladder. She was so overweight she couldn't rise from the splits without assistance from the audience. We had quite a weekend with her at the Aragon Club in Peterborough, a restaurant and bar won by its proprietor, Jack Weinstein, in a poker game and, after a few years, lost by him in another poker game. Weinstein got so many complaints about Kitty Carr's inept dancing on Friday that he complained to her agent, who sent in Amazing Grace for Saturday.

Amazing Grace stepped off the bus under a wide-brimmed pink hat two hours before she was to hit the stage and told us she needed no rehearsal. "You know how to play 'Brazil'? Fine. Just play 'Brazil' ... fast." Which we did. She had fearsome confidence, and though we pounded out a furious tempo, she calmly faced me on the crowded stage and chewed gum.

I hollered, "Is something wrong"?

But she merely shrugged and slowly ground her rear at the patrons until their faces twisted with her, riveted to her every motion. They grinned, slapped their foreheads, and before she finished gave her a standing ovation. Only later did we learn she had drawn eyes and a moustache on her supple buttocks and mimicked Groucho Marx. "But why to 'Brazil'?" I asked her later.

"Shut up," she explained.

The night wasn't over. We still had Kitty Carr. And before intermission a man with only one leg, on crutches, jumped over three chairs laid out onstage. Gus Karakas was actually a friend of ours, a wealthy businessman from Sudbury who often turned up unannounced at our shows. As a boy, he had lost a leg under a train, but rose above his handicap to skate in an ice show and jump nine barrels. He suspected we doubted his claim, and so that night to settle disbelief and upstage Amazing Grace to boot he decided the time had come. Gus couldn't do the nine barrels anymore, but the three chairs would give him credence. And it was indeed quite a feat, considering he was now middle-aged, rotund, out of practice, and drunk.

Charlie Rush announced what Gus was about to do, and I gave him a roll on the drums. He came clumping out of the smoking gloom, leaped two steps onto the stage, floated for a moment in the spotlights over the chairs, and disappeared into the gloom on the other side. His crutches stood straight up where he had released them and fell in slow motion as he hopped on one leg with a thunderous crash into a table loaded with beer. He drew as much applause as Amazing Grace.

80

Super Seniors Pass the Torch

The continuing distress over students having to walk not quite two miles from Clement Mill and Chimney Hill subdivisions to Galt Collegiate Institute touches off a chorus of howls from old-timers about how far they had to walk to school. In retrospect the distances extend and we get sworn testimony from people who walked on crutches in the freezing rain to Dr. Tassie's school from as far out as Sheffield.

I remember my father frothing on about the blizzards he crawled through to the little old schoolhouse in Haysville and to the army recruiting office in New Dundee. His harangues matured me so that I vowed never to boast to a younger generation about how far I walked to school. *It was two miles.* We wouldn't walk *kilometres* in those days. However, let's put the past under the bridge with everything else and try to inspire today's young rabble with examples of our outstanding seniors.

Take Art Wilson, for instance. All through his sixties he jogged ten miles every morning before the kids were out of bed. That's like running to GCI from Clyde and back nonstop. In Buffalo, where he ran in the big marathons, he was named *Buffalo News* Runner of the Year. Now that he's over eighty he's limited to running up the 1,760 steps of the CN Tower in Toronto to raise money for the United Way.

And how about Super Ron Osborne of Cambridge Memorial Hospital? He walked two miles a day to work at the hospital (a four-mile round trip) five days a week for twenty-four years. One thousand miles a year, once around the Earth since he started. He never owned a car, and the buses weren't running when he set off at 5:00 a.m. And when he got to work he pitched forty-pound bags of soiled linen into carts that eventually weighed over 600 pounds as he hauled them around the halls. He said the walk home burnt off the tension. His greatest walking feat resulted from an aborted bus trip home from a country-and-western pilgrimage

164

to the United States. Super Ron's bus from Buffalo was too late to connect with his bus from Hamilton to Galt, so he had to walk home — twenty-five miles! He left Hamilton at midnight and marched into Galt at 7:00 a.m. But then he was only fifty-eight years old.

Nobody, however, can surpass Stuart Park. You've probably passed him in his yellow-and-orange safety jacket walking along the Brantford highway. The police gave him the safety jacket after drivers reported almost running him over. Each working day from age ninety to ninety-three he hitchhiked from his home on Highway 5, a mile west of Osborne's Corner, to his job at the Tiger Brand plant on Melville Street in Galt. There he was a sweeper, general utility man, and an inspiration to everyone, especially the ladies on the third floor with whom he flirted. He worked at Tiger Brand until 3:00 p.m. and then walked up Main Street to the Ontario Conservatory of Music where he put in another hour of cleaning. That done he walked a mile to the Concession Street Bridge where he donned his safety jacket for the hitchhike home.

"Working at Tiger Brand keeps me young," he would say. "Puts a tiger in my tank. It's the best job I've ever had. I sure hope they don't ask me to take early retirement." If you gave him a ride, he would sing you a song from the 1920s. He's retired from this world now, and I miss him.

81

The Inspiration of Art Wilson

On a Sunday morning in 1992 I rose not long after the sun and drove to the Footbridge off Highway 24 south of Galt. I wasn't thinking of jumping off. I was on a secret mission.

Parked at the east end of the bridge, I scanned the highway to the north through my binoculars. Nothing moved except turkey vultures and a woman picking beer bottles out of the ditch. At last, on the brow of the hill, a figure in an iridescent jogging suit bobbed into view. It was Art Wilson, out for his ten-miler.

Art had been on the brow of the hill for a long time. He was sixty-eight. In his prime he ran with such notable runners as Ab Morton and Scotty Rankine. Rankine was voted Canada's athlete of the year in 1935 and won the Norton H. Grove Trophy in 1937 as Canada's top amateur athlete. So Art was no longer out to set records. He was out to inspire younger men to set records. That morning he was on a training run. His two trainees had given him a three-minute head start and were catching up fast. By the time he reached my car, he was looking over his shoulder as if he were John Landy watching for Roger Bannister. Half a mile back his trainees appeared on the horizon, and so that they wouldn't see my car, I drove to the west side of the bridge.

Art came huffing over the bridge and piled into the passenger seat. "They haven't seen us," he said, and pressed a finger to his wrist. "Pulse eighty-one. Now that's fitness for you. I have the triglycerides of a man of thirty-two."

"How far do you want me to drive you?" I asked.

"Just around the bend, far enough to keep them out of sight."

Art didn't want his trainees to become complacent. They always caught up with him, and he was afraid they might lose their competitive fire.

He got out of the car around the bend and headed for Grandridge Hill. What a hill! I wasn't sure the car could make it, but Art ran it. "I never cheat on a hill," he told me. Through the binoculars I picked up one of the trainees far below, opening his throttle, tongue lolling, eyes bugging, and an incredulous look on his face. At the brow of the hill Art climbed into the car again. "If you think this is physical fitness," he gasped, "wait until I peak in a couple of months." Just looking at him sent my pulse staggering past his.

When Art got out of the car once more on St. Andrews Street, a man walking his dog stared and smiled. I hollered to him not to tell the runners following what he had seen. "That's the second time I've seen him get out of a car," the man said, sealing his lips with a finger. His dog wagged its tail.

Trainee Kirk Oliver caught up with Art before he passed the YMCA at Queen's Square. He had seen the car. But trainee Pete Harth was too far back to spot the scam. He didn't catch up until Art was practising shallow breathing in front of his house on Kerr Street. The perspiration towelled from his face and his pulse slowed to about ten, Art greeted Pete with nonchalance. "Can't catch the old master every time, Pete," he said.

To help me unwind after such a long drive, Art served me tea in his recreation room where the weight of medals on the wall threatened to pull the house down. "Someday," he said, "those two guys will be hopping into cars to inspire their trainees."

"Which race do you consider your best, Art?" I asked.

"The next one," he said. It would be years before he was confined to running up the CN Tower.

82

Ben Graham — Poet at Heart

If Ben Graham hadn't taken sixty-five years off from his writing career to raise a family, he might have become a Canadian icon of the stature of Mordecai Richler or Peter Gzowski. But now we'll never know, because he passed away in 2001 at ninety-four.

In the 1920s Ben was a hot-blooded romantic who toyed with tossing his job in Goldie's Pattern Works and thumbing his way to Greenwich Village in New York City to seek out Edna St. Vincent Millay. She, too, was a hot-blooded romantic and had just won the Pulitzer Prize for *The Harp-Weaver and Other Poems*. Ben had also written some poems and had published them in the *Reporter* under a pseudonym. It was then considered unmanly to write poetry, and he didn't want to be teased by his workmates at the pattern works.

Ben's dream to meet Millay dissolved one night in Port Dover when he met his wife-to-be at a jitney dance in the Summer Gardens. Jitney dancing was a form of metred sin. You paid 5 cents to waltz your girl for one number. Then ushers cleared the floor with a rope and you had to pay another 5 cents to get back on for the next number. Ben was dancing with a neat-looking girl when, over her shoulder, he spotted a better one on the sideline. She turned out to be his dancing partner's sister. Five cents later he was dancing with an intelligent and spirited beauty of Ukrainian descent. He so liked the idea of landing such a catch for 5 cents that he married her. But this meant working for a living.

He worked for Ontario Hydro in various capacities for more than forty years and didn't turn his pen to poetry and prose again until long after he retired and his wife had died. By then he was eighty-nine. Clyde Warrington, an editor at the *Reporter*, got him to write a weekly column, which he did for two years. In that brief time Ben wrote more than 30,000 words that were read and enjoyed. He got fan mail from California and an offer to write for a newspaper in the Maritimes.

In his youth Ben lived with his strict Presbyterian parents in Galt at the foot of Augusta Street, close to the Grand River. On hot summer nights he slept on the front porch, but often, after midnight, he would awaken, sneak down to the river, and swim in the inky blackness over to Devil's Cave on the far bank and back. His parents never found out.

The girls in his Sunday school class at Central Church were almost his age and loved to tease him with embarrassing questions. One girl asked him what (thou shalt not commit) adultery was. He blushed and said, "I don't know exactly, but I can tell you it's worse than shoplifting ..."

I first met Ben at his ninetieth birthday party in his garden in Waterloo. His daughter, Maxine, a noted theatre set designer, had organized the party and surrounded her father with people from the arts with whom he identified. Ben had a late-life career with the hospitals in Kitchener. He laboured with a pacemaker on his heart and asthma in his lungs, and it got so that if you wanted to talk to him you had to follow his ambulance. On and off for two years he livened up the wards with his tape recordings of Guy Lombardo and Leon Bismark "Bix" Beiderbecke, one of the great alcoholic jazz cornet players of the 1920s.

Although he was brought up by strict Presbyterians, Ben evolved into a humanist. A lot of people, including Erika Kubassek, prayed mightily for his soul, so it will be interesting to discover where he wound up when the line moves forward and it's my turn to go. *Next*.

83

Historic Toilet Seat

*O*ld artists never fade away. They have too much fun flirting with death. Some seniors set dubious examples, but are fearless nonetheless.

Every time I pass the little cottage at 134 Swan Street in Ayr, I wonder what happened to the rear porch toilet seat embedded with the American Civil War musket ball. A strange icon, but not when you consider who owned the house when the mystical event occurred.

John Martin, one of Canada's most underrated artists, bought the house in the 1950s because he claimed it was the oldest home in Ayr. He was obsessed with antiquity and painted many historically significant buildings in the area. Martin was a meticulous craftsman and filled his barn-studio next to his house with what appeared to be blueprints of every building he had painted. He was also an American Civil War aficionado and spent a lot of time searching and sketching the ruins of the battlefields south of the border. That was the cause of much raucous debate with his friend Carl Schaefer, another artist of note and a Civil War buff. Schaefer had sketched the ruin of a stone bridge near Gettysburg with three arches. Martin, on the basis of his research, painted it with four. They both loved to drink and shout every disputed detail of the war at the top of their lungs. Often when neither could validate a historical point they would burst into song — really bawdy ones.

Schaefer lived near Toronto and taught at the Ontario College of Art. Martin taught at Ridley College near St. Catharines. Both have works in the National Gallery. They got together at Martin's house in Ayr about once a month. Between visits they debated by mail, illustrating their postal envelopes with cartoons of each other duelling with sword and musket and shouting ribald hints about what to find inside.

Schaefer always embellished his envelopes with a Nazi swastika postal stamp that he picked up in Germany during World War II. He was a war artist, and more than 100 of his paintings hang in the Canadian War Museum in Ottawa. On one of his envelopes Schaefer painted a map of Gettysburg to illustrate an error Martin had made in their last debate. Some of the obscenities on their envelopes were censored by the post office with black ink.

Martin loved to sit in his back sunroom and gaze over a yard that rolled unfenced out to the Nith River flats, which teemed with butterflies and ghosts. He was particularly fond of an old cherry tree at the foot of the yard, which he claimed on most mornings hosted half a dozen pheasants.

On a trip to the United States, Martin bought an authentic Civil War musket. Not to be outdone, Schaefer turned up with a bag of black powder and a Civil War musket ball he had dug out of the battlefield at Antietam Creek. Needless to say, they had to fire the musket. Martin couldn't imagine a nicer resting place for the musket ball than the trunk of his old cherry tree. Schaefer concurred because he said he couldn't afford the legal consequences of firing it into Martin.

After priming and loading the musket, they flipped a coin to decide who should have the honour of firing it. Schaefer won. However, in his shaky hands, the gun fired before he could properly take aim, and the ball went through the thin wooden wall of Martin's sunroom. Martin ran inside to see where it went and spotted a ragged hole, two feet off the floor, through the plywood wall of the lavatory.

"Are you in there, Agnes?" he hollered to his wife. She wasn't, and he barged in. There was no sign of the musket ball except the hole beside the toilet seat. And sure enough, there it was, lodged neatly in the wooden rim. "That's where she stays," he announced. He liked that better than the cherry tree. "I've got the only toilet seat in the world embedded with an authentic U.S. Civil War musket ball." Schaefer liked it, too, and they drank to it.

Martin was killed by a drunken driver near Ayr in the 1960s, but Schaefer soldiered on to die of wear and tear in 1995 at ninety-three. The people who bought Martin's house didn't know about the musket ball in the toilet seat, and when they were told about it, they couldn't find it. But then they had a new seat. The old one had disappeared. Could it be in the Canadian War Museum in Ottawa?

84
Victor's Out the Window

The generation gap closes in show business, and in the theatre rising young stars are regularly upstaged by actors in their dotage, especially when they're drunk. Anyone who has been to a Little Theatre drama festival knows the best performances are at the reception following the award ceremony. I recall vividly a Western Ontario Drama League reception in the mid-1960s at the old Oxford Hotel in Woodstock. I didn't attend the drama festival but was playing in a band at the lovely Copacabana Nightclub right behind the hotel.

To digress a bit, the Copa was Woodstock's first and possibly last Vegas-style nightclub, peculiar enough to attract farmhands in corn caps from the Oxford Hotel beer parlour to ogle the entrance.

The management had done the place over in wrought-iron Spanish on red carpet, the wrought-iron chairs too heavy to move and bristling with crooks that snagged dresses and pockets so that one could hear the ripping of cloth over the music. One man ripped his pocket far enough around that you could see his striped undershorts.

Anyway, the Saturday night of the drama festival a boisterous crowd of actors swept in and made the club feel for a while like the real Copa in New York City. Some actors from Galt invited me back to the reception at the Oxford after my job ended. The reception was in a large room on the second floor of the hotel, towards the rear, above where the stables used to be. The best lungs in London, Kitchener, Woodstock, Owen Sound, and Windsor were on hard, and they were "projecting," as the voice trainer would say, like a tree full of starlings.

Audrey Vale of Galt trumpeted away, like Tallulah Bankhead, to Rick Crossey, who blasted back loud enough to crack the plaster on the walls, thoroughly enjoying themselves without noticing a single word the other said. To my discomfort, smiling and with a drink in his hand, there was T.H. Wholton, my stern old high school principal who used to suspend me for oft-repeated truancy. And then there was Margaret Fraser, also from Galt Collegiate Institute, who wouldn't tolerate a whisper or snigger in her library. "Green!" she hollered, addressing me still in classroom protocol, "can I get you a drink?"

Although it was March, the room was terribly hot and most of the windows were open. At one window a gay little man who looked like a penguin in his tux, perched on the sill and fenced with his glass at passersby. He was an adjudicator — in his cups and in his seventies.

I didn't see him go, but I heard a women shriek, "Victor's out the window!"

The noise stopped as if the hotel had hit an iceberg. Then a man shouted, "For God's sake, don't anyone tell the manager!" After that the crowd rushed for the stairs.

There was a foot-long drop from the windowsill to a sloping corrugated metal roof. A trough in the wet snow betrayed where a body had slid down and dropped into the darkness above the rear parking lot. Victor had cruised slowly down on his back and plopped gently onto the roof of a car in a soggy cushion of snow. From there he climbed to the ground, glass still in hand, and headed back around to the front entrance. Except for the slush in his pants he was unscathed. He slogged up to the entrance just as the crowd, led by a man dressed like the duke of Clarence, burst shrieking into the street.

"What's wrong?" Victor asked.

"A man has fallen out a window."

"Well, isn't that strange?" Victor said. "The same thing just happened to me."

And he ran with the rest of them to the back of the hotel to see what had happened to himself.

85

An Old Shaggy Drunk

I've known some funny old dogs, notably one who drank beer and socialized in Nicholson's Inn in Blair. It wouldn't be fair to remember Nicholson's Inn only for its motorcycle gangs, fist-fights on neighbours' lawns, and deafening rock music. There were times when Nicks offered the serenity of a cathedral, where one could find peace and quiet and privacy, even darkness at noon.

I'm thinking of the Fireside Lounge on a weekday when the shades were always drawn so that when you entered from the sunlight there was such darkness that the place seemed to be closed. There was just enough dim light from the bar lights to guide you to the placemats on the tables. It took a minute or two after you sat down to realize you weren't alone. You heard a muffled cough or clink of a glass. Then the shadows began to move and eyes peered back from the silhouettes of some of Galt's and Kitchener's most venturesome businessmen. The silhouettes of their secretaries took another minute to register. They were very quiet, as silhouettes are wont to be, and no trouble to the village at all, though I understand their presence here caused a lot of noise at home.

Occasionally, while you wondered with whom you shared the darkness, you were startled by a big wet tongue licking your hand. This wasn't one of the secretaries out of control, but Kelly Kirkwood, a large old Gordon setter who belonged to Dave Kirkwood, who lived a short distance up the road. Kelly often ambled over to the inn on his own. Someone always opened the door for him, and he would settle in for a few languid hours of social drinking. He must have been a major domo in another life at one of the better resorts because he went from table to table wagging his tail, was a good listener, and felt at ease drinking with the clientele.

The regulars called for a clean ashtray and poured him a draft. After he slurped it up and wagged his tail, he sidled over to another table to lick another hand. He never caused a commotion aside from barking once when he wanted to go outside to the john. He didn't drink and drive, either. Whenever he got a bit wobbly, the bar manager called Dave Kirkwood to come and pick him up. "Kelly," Dave would say, "how many times have I told you?" as, like a chauffeur, he held open the car door for Kelly to hop in.

It was my privilege to drive Kelly home twice, once late at night when he was really sloshed. I had to shoulder him into the front seat. There he sat, taller than I, his shaggy soccer-ball-sized head sagging forward to pant alcoholic mist on the windshield and fill the car with a miasma of beer fumes. Suddenly, I realized what a predicament I would be in if I encountered one of the police's frequent spot checks for intoxicated drivers at the village limits. As soon as I rolled down the window, the officer would smell the beer and invite me out to walk the line.

"But, Officer, it's not me. It's my passenger … Kelly. He's a dog."

"Yeah."

86
A Visit with Pratt

Before we leave seniors and remember old people who refused to grow up, I must recount my last visit with Phil Pratt who, as a virtuoso with his moving van (he billed himself as Pratt the Mover … the Gentle Giant), his trumpet and dance band, and his hospital portering, made more acquaintances than the governor general. After he retired from the hospital, he walked around downtown Galt daily, chatting with everyone and putting smiles on their faces. They missed him sorely after he moved to Terrance Park Lodge in Brantford.

Pratt wanted to treat me to a coffee. We walked from the lodge across Dalhousie Street where cars pass like artillery shells, through a small shaded park, across Colborne Street where the artillery shells

174

pass in the opposite direction, to Poppy's Wobbly Bar and Grill, a hospitable little oasis frequented by what former New Democratic Party leader Ed Broadbent fondly refers to as "ordinary people."

I insisted on treating Pratt because he had treated me on our last visit. He said no, that I had treated him and it was only fair for him to take his turn. We both put change on the table, but he pushed mine back and paid with his. The coffees totalled $1.60. The waitress, befuddled by our shuffling of change, returned after a few minutes and put down $1.40. Pratt pushed it across to me. It's yours. You paid."

"No, you paid," I said. "And there shouldn't be any change." The waitress rolled her eyes, smiled, and walked away.

To avoid further argument, Pratt said we should go halves and pushed half of the change towards me. He palmed his half into a tiny leather pouch.

Pratt asked me when I was born. I told him 1930. "I was born in 1920," he said, adding that he had been a widower a decent enough length of time to consider dating again, but it would be difficult to replace Nora and he would bide his time. The lady of his choice had to be between seventy-five and ninety, a nonsmoker, capable of making it across Dalhousie Street to the Wobbly Bar without stress incontinence, able to take turns paying the bill, and be experienced at fending off aggressive dogs with her walker.

Our conversation digressed like a ball in a pinball machine. We talked about mutual acquaintances, musicians who had fallen down stairs, and ladies who might give us trouble. I told him the story of the bass fiddle player, a friend of bass fiddle player Bob Milne, who plunged down a flight of stairs with a bottle of 100-proof rum in his jacket pocket. Feeling his shirt soaked after he crashed on the landing, he cried out, "Please, God, let it be blood."

Before we left Wobbly's, Pratt walked up to the bar and dumped all the change from his pouch. "I want to pay for two coffees," he said. The bartender smiled and said we had already paid. Pratt looked at me and asked, "Did you pay again?"

"No," I said. "You paid ... I think."

The bartender chuckled and said, "Let's just say somebody paid. Watch your step crossing the road."

Pratt presented the bartender with two quarters and said, "There's a tip for being honest."

The bartender took the coins and said, "I'll put it towards your next coffee."

"Next time," Pratt said, "it's on me."

87

Too Busy to Grow Old Quietly

A few of us refuse to become seniors but instead grow old riotously. Vart Vartanian comes to mind.

Most Galtonians have Vart Vartanian stories to tell, but few people can adequately describe him. To call him ebullient strains the meaning of the word. Vart was a wild boy from the day he was born until the day he died at seventy-eight. He was emotionally disinhibited, physically powerful, and fast enough to whip any three men in a fistfight, yet gentle and generous to the point of foolishness, an astonishingly handsome womanizer, a consummate freestyle jazz dancer, and a person so trusted and admired that once, in the 1950s, when a misdemeanour landed him in jail in Utah, Canon Thomas of Trinity Anglican Church and the mayor of Galt exerted their influence to have him set free and sent home.

Vart introduced the zoot suit to Galt, that monster of postwar excess with the voluminous chest-high trousers, knee-length jacket with cantilevered shoulders, four-foot looping chain, and squat fedora with six-inch rim. He sported it proudly up and down Main Street, though the trouser tops chafed his armpits.

Perhaps one story to which I can attest will shed some light on part of Vart's nature. Willis Toles (the terror of Harold Gray's funeral home) and I were driving to Buffalo one Sunday in the early 1960s to indulge in the afternoon jazz sessions at the black musicians' union local on Genosese Street. At Peters' Corners we spotted Vart hitchhiking. He, too, was going to Buffalo. A girlfriend there had mailed him $10 for bus fare, but he had chosen to save it and hitchhike.

Crossing through customs at the border was always an adventure with Toles, but with Vart added it became preposterous. Asked what he had to declare, Toles declared he was the world's greatest trombone player and proceeded to get his horn out of its case to prove it. The customs officers stopped him. There was a lineup behind us. Mr. Vartanian, Toles said, was the ambassador to Canada from Armenia who was visiting the United States to give a jazz-dancing demonstration at a cultural centre on Genosese Street. "He's been in jail, too," Toles added, hollering now. The customs officers waved us through.

At the jazz club Vart was every inch the ambassador from Armenia, treating black gangsters to drinks with his $10 and refraining from flirting with their white girlfriends. After the afternoon session, we were invited to play with the combo at Duff's Sheridan Patio in east Buffalo. As fate would have it, there had been a jazz-dancing contest there that day and the winning contestants demonstrated their top number while the combo played.

Vart was unleashed. At the end of the demonstration he politely took hold of the winning contestant's partner and commenced to dance what he hollered was the Limpopo. The combo matched his pace with a fast mambo. Vart scissored his legs and lashed out with his arms as if he were boxing the whole crowd. He spun his partner until her eyes crossed, then flung her up, over, and around like the Gyro ride at the midway. The crowd began to stamp and hoot. Clearly, he would have won the contest that afternoon. There was thunderous applause.

Later a waitress came to the bandstand to present "to the boys from Canada" three bottles of wine in Christmas wrappings (it was August). Toles and I got ours, but Vart failed to come to the stand when called. He had disappeared with his dance partner. I don't know how he got home.

88

Janet of Swamp Angel Street

Janet Elliott was my friend who grew up the least. Her consummate compassion for people and animals blocked any hope for an orderly life, a tidy home, a cent in the bank, or time to become sedate.

I mentioned her earlier as one of the little girls on the wooden bridge who had their skirts blown up by the steam locomotives. She was then Janet Winter.

In her twenties she taught elementary school for a while but dared to switch to a taxing and chaotic career as props department manager for the largest television commercial production company in Toronto — The Partners. In her fifties she forfeited this job to return to Galt to care for her dying mother and maiden aunt, Elizabeth McHoul. Before her mother died Janet promised to care for "Auntie," as she called Elizabeth, so that the woman would never have to enter a nursing home. Auntie was then seventy-nine. Janet was also raising a teenage son, Lorne, the product of a failed marriage.

After her mother died, Janet moved Auntie and Lorne and many pet animals into an old railway station in St. George, the waiting room of which she converted into an antique shop. This enterprise failed, and she sold the property and moved everyone into a house in the village on what the locals called Swamp Angel Street. She then became the spare clerk, ice-cream scooper, and waitress for every shop and restaurant in the village.

Janet tried to keep track of her commitments with memos. Memos about job days switched, money owed to her, money she owed, people needing cats and dogs, and people in need of her advice. Memos sprouted from her cigarette packs and filled her purse. Out-of-date memos covered her fridge door, the door to the living room, the door to the porch, and the bottom half of her kitchen cupboard doors.

Memos from the previous year's calendar were pinned down on counters by conch shells, a Royal Doulton mug sporting the face of Field Marshal Bernard Montgomery, a model steam locomotive made of chocolate, and back issues of *Good Housekeeping*. Janet wrote herself memos to sort and discard old memos, and they, too, joined the piles.

She taught herself to frame pictures and, reminded by a memo, matted and framed a large print for a hairdresser in Brantford who became her confidant and drinking partner and trimmed her hair for free. Janet had no car, but a memo reminded her to call me to help her deliver the print. A memo reminding her that he wasn't home that day fell from her cigarette pack when we parked in front of his house.

To avoid a return trip we searched for a safe place to leave the print. A tool shed with door ajar at the foot of his yard seemed the best repository, and she jotted a memo to leave in his door. After climbing a five-foot board fence topped by three strands of barbed wire, I took the print from Janet's hands and tiptoed towards the shed through a minefield of large dog turds, fighting strong gusts of wind that caught the print like a sail and threatened to tip me over. Halfway to the shed, I heard the dogs, three of them with different pitched barks, slavering and hurling themselves against the glass patio doors. The hairdresser was gay, had been beaten by hooligans, and acquired the most savage dogs for protection. One of them, I discerned through the perspiration stinging my eyes, was a pit bull.

"If they break through the door," Janet hollered, "don't run because they can smell fear."

Immediately, I ran for the shed, thrust the print inside and, flapping my arms like a loon seeking to be airborne, sprinted through the dog turds and cleared the fence with just one nick in my hand.

"Why are you laughing?" I asked. "I risked my life in there."

"You looked so funny," she said. "But not to worry. You've done a good turn. Doesn't that make you proud?"

Janet had four dogs of her own and an uncertain number of cats, all strays. Two of her dogs had only three legs. One of them, a tiny white mutt she named Tripod, always sported red lipstick imprints on his forehead. Janet regularly walked Tripod on a leash over to Twinklebones Restaurant on the main street for a saucer of warm milk.

Twinklebones Restaurant was owned and managed by Tom Parry, a Welshman, and his Irish wife, Mae. It was the Moulin Rouge of St. George, a haven for middle-aged hippies, antique dealers, itinerant musicians, and members of drama clubs. Twinklebones had no liquor licence, but liberated ladies from neighbouring towns, modish and affecting large hats, often met there for afternoon tea and to chat about the theatre, baking, and perversions while sipping straight rum from fine china teacups.

On special nights, especially St. Patrick's and Robbie Burns's Days, the place was packed until the floors sagged. There was entertainment. A troupe billed as the Bullshit Ballet, two women entangled in lace and two men in purple tights, plunged and kicked inanely around the tables to *The Nutcracker* on a stereo. Janet, of course, was one of the women in lace. I saw her, dancing, pop an orange from her bra and hit Len Iseler on the head. Then, as she whirled by my chair, she confided loudly, "If I didn't do this, I'd go crazy." She also sat on a counter and sang "Slow Boat to China" through a toilet paper roll.

Auntie lived on and on, her pension cheque crucial to everyone's survival. She had great Presbyterian faith, but often called the Lord to order. When there wasn't enough money on hand to pay the mortgage, she would say, "I wish the Lord would step in."

In her late eighties Auntie began to have annual medical disasters. They began at the old railway station, situated at the foot of a steep lane, and always in the winter when the lane was drifted shut with snow. She had to be bundled up and pushed up through the drifts by teams of people led by Lorne with a shovel. Auntie was large. These efforts are remembered like military campaigns: Auntie's renal failure of 1984, her pneumonia of 1987 and 1988, the great fall down the stairs of 1989, and several minor strokes. Each time the doctors gave her little chance of survival and each time she rebounded to return to Twinklebones for a hearty meal. During this time, Janet was also nursing her older brother, Donald Winter, through his long siege of terminal cancer. He didn't make the move to Swamp Angel Street.

One night in the spring of 1991 Janet phoned me at 11:00 p.m. to say that Auntie had passed on.

"How do you know?" I asked.

"She is dead still on her bed and not breathing."

180

"Have you checked her pulse?"

"I'm afraid to touch her. I don't know what to do. Could you call Vic Corbett for me?"

Vic Corbett was then still in charge of Corbett's Funeral Home in Galt. From the day he started the business I sold him more than a dozen prints of paintings of Galt, Preston, and Hespeler. They proved popular, and he asked me for more. All I had was one of the main street of St. George. He liked the print but declined to buy it because he said he got no business from St. George. With Auntie in mind I asked him if he might buy the print if I got him a client from there. He agreed and we shook hands.

So that night I called him at home and said, "Vic, remember our deal on the client from St. George? Well, it's happened."

He said okay and offered the advice Janet needed — phone the coroner, get the death certificate and so on, and leave the rest up to Corbett's. "Tell her there's nothing to worry about."

Janet was much relieved when I called back but wondered if I would drive down to help. Lorne was away and she was scared. When I got there, she was standing just inside the front door. She didn't say anything. I suggested we go upstairs and look at Auntie. She said no, not yet, that Auntie was on the john.

"On the john!" I said. "How can she be dead if she's on the john?"

"You don't know these Presbyterians."

We heard the toilet flush. Auntie had gotten off her bed right after Janet hung up the phone, and she was too mortified to call me back. I went home.

The next morning I drove back to see how things were and found Janet and Auntie in Twinklebones Restaurant. Auntie was eating hastily because she had to run next door for a hair appointment. So I called Corbett's. "Vic," I said, "better put the St. George print on the back burner because I just had lunch with the client." Vic was a good sport and bought the print, anyway.

The next year, 1992, Auntie fooled everyone and passed away peacefully at age ninety-seven.

In the spring of 1993 a lovely lady named Alison Caron, whom Janet under dire circumstances had given up for adoption thirty-nine years before while she was still attending normal school, came down from Timmins to meet her mother for the first time and present her with three charming granddaughters: Kate, ten; Olivia, eight; and Grace, four. Janet was ecstatic. She was also exhausted by it all, by everything over the years, and on April 14, 1994, passed on herself at age sixty-two. A lot of people cried. She was the angel of Swamp Angel Street.

89
Cliffhanging with IMAX

I, did have friends who were organized, but even they had some close calls.

IMAX Systems Corporation, which introduced the world to 70 mm film projected onto sixty-foot-high screens, had its roots in Galt where it was preceded by a small film company in the 1960s founded by Graeme Ferguson and Robert Kerr, classmates at Galt Collegiate Institute.

The 70 mm camera and projector were still dreams whose development depended largely on the financial success of a more conventional 35 mm film entitled *Polar Life* to be projected on multi-screens at the Man in the Polar Regions Pavilion at Expo 67 in Montreal during Canada's Centennial Year.

Much of the success of this film resulted from breathtaking views of Ellesmere Island in our Far North, really frightening views as seen through Ferguson's cameras in the nose of a chartered twin-engine Piper as it skimmed suicidally up and down the ragged glaciers. After the pilot completed a few of these runs, one of the plane's engines coughed out and the pilot announced that to make it home all possible weight had to be pitched overboard.

The first to go was a large, heavy toolbox. Next were the seats, which had to be ripped out with desperation because the wrenches to loosen them had gone first with the toolbox. During this frantic effort, a crew member tossed out his money and passport. The cameras had to go, too — thousands of dollars' worth, Ferguson's and Kerr's life savings. But the film was saved and, lightened just enough, the plane limped back to base. Upon landing the first thing Ferguson did, after kissing the tarmac as if he were the pope, was phone his office in Montreal to file an insurance claim covering the camera equipment.

The tiny office was run by a single woman. After she got Ferguson's call, she realized to her horror that she had forgotten to renew the insurance policy. In desperation she called the insurance company and discovered that the clerk handling the policy had forgotten to cancel it. So to cover his error and hers he honoured the policy, and IMAX wasn't stillborn on Ellesmere Island.

Twenty years later Robert Kerr chanced upon a prospector, Ross Toms, who had spent much of his life working the area around Baffin Island. He talked about the Inuit and their customs and how they had been of great help to him in his prospecting. Funny thing, though, he said, the Inuit had no particular interest in mineral prospecting, but they were obsessed by a search of their own for objects as mysterious and treasured as the Holy Grail. They told a story of a supposed aircraft that had dropped some exotic photographic treasures into the deep snows of a glacier and that whoever found them would be very rich. Toms had no knowledge of Kerr's near disaster over Ellesmere Island. The Inuit are to this day still searching and embellishing the legend of the lost treasure. But if they find the stuff, will anybody tip off the insurance company?

One day a few years after the adventure on Ellesmere Island, Graeme Ferguson drove me down to McMaster University where, in a rented industrial lab, Bill Shaw had just rescued IMAX from another disaster, this time with his wife's small Hoover vacuum cleaner.

IMAX at the time had entered into a contract with a large Japanese firm to demonstrate the 70 mm projector in a pavilion at Expo 70 in Osaka. However, with a deadline just two weeks away, the projector, Bill Shaw's creation, refused to function properly. The 70 mm film, with ten times the area of conventional 35 mm film, tended to ripple every time a frame stopped at the projector gate.

Of course, you can't project movies onto screens as high as the Canadian Pacific Railway bridge in Galt with ripples running across the image. Shaw tried to stop the ripples, shock waves really, by pressing the film in a liquid between two sheets of glass. No luck. But one night at 2:00 a.m. he awoke from a fitful sleep and wondered if "suction" would hold the film flat.

Shaw slipped out of bed and rushed down to the lab with his wife's little Hoover, the small cylindrical type on runners that you tow over the carpet. He rigged the vacuum hose to the projector gate and ran a film. Eureka! (Not the vacuum.) It worked. No ripples. And with amazingly little suction.

When Graeme and I got to the lab, Bill, still euphoric and in high gear, was demonstrating the projector to technicians from the Link Trainer Company who were seeking virtual reality simulation for student pilots. He was projecting a film of a charging rhinoceros that Graeme had shot in Africa for a Lowell Thomas television series. The improvised screen was a large sheet of white paper taped to the wall. As the rhino charged closer, the image definition became so acute that one could see flies landing and taking off from the beast's horn.

The projector itself was an awesome animal. Its light source came from a sort of bulb that National Aeronautics and Space Administration (NASA) in the United States used to test materials for the effects of gamma rays. In the projector the dangerous rays had to be screened through a large quartz crystal, and its volcanic heat was dispersed by powerful fans through an octopus of furnace pipes. Enough heat still leaked through the projector lens to cause a fence board passed within a foot to burst into flames. The film ran on reels as large as manhole covers, lay horizontally, and was fed through the gate like a typewriter ribbon. This complexity caused the projector to weigh eleven tons and sit on four stout legs like a lunar landing craft. Atop this monster sat Barbara Shaw's tiny green Hoover, its vacuum hose stretched to the gate. An industrial vacuum accompanied the projector to Osaka where its performance introduced IMAX to the world. This original projector was installed in Ontario Place and might still be there.

Bill Shaw, Graeme Ferguson, and Robert Kerr, the holy trinity of IMAX, went through Galt Collegiate Institute in the same class, and it was their mutual respect that caused Shaw to leave his secure position as chief bicycle engineer for CCM to risk all for his friends and their revolutionary cinematic project. He knew nothing about cameras or projectors, but soon, as his partners knew he would, he became a world authority in the field. Graeme Ferguson's brother-in-law, Roman Kroitor, left the National Film Board to become the fourth indispensable member of the team.

IMAX succeeded, and its founders carried it as far as their energies would allow before selling it off for a handsome profit. All of them are rich and three of them are socialists.

It's a measure of the power of the large screen that it succeeded on documentaries. IMAX's new owners are now converting to commercial films that might conceivably render the small screens of multiplex cinemas obsolete.

Unfortunately, Bill Shaw won't see this phase of the cinematic revolution in which he played such a crucial role. He died suddenly in September 2002 at seventy-three. He came from Hespeler.

90
Consider a Miracle

It's time for a miracle story. I don't believe in them, but here is one, anyway, as told to me by Mary Dinniwell one day when I was visiting her at Fairview Mennonite Home. She was eighty-nine and her wandering mind was doing the talking. For a while she spoke about the new water-saving toilets being installed at Fairview. As a conservationist, she thought they were wonderful. Their only fault, she said, was that you had to flush them twice. Then she drifted off on a more ethereal current to a time and place where there were no flush toilets.

Mrs. Dinniwell's grandfather, Adam Glazier, was a Methodist missionary on the Cape Croker Reserve on the Bruce Peninsula north of Wiarton, Ontario, in the 1870s when Georgian Bay was shrouded in legends, mysticism, blizzards, and fog. All provisions for the small settlement came by boat except in the winter when everything had to be dragged across the treacherous ice.

On a sunny day in July a small steamer anchored offshore to unload provisions, and everyone in the settlement, as was the custom, came down to the stony beach to greet it. A young minister and his wife, on board the steamer en route to a church summer camp on Christian Island, decided upon seeing the crowd on the beach to go ashore and visit while the boat was unloading. The captain lowered a skiff for them. They had to descend to the skiff on a rope ladder. The young minister went first and guided his wife, who was carrying a tiny baby, bundled and asleep. As he was about to take the baby from her arms, she stepped onto the gunnel of the skiff, and their combined weight on that side flipped it over and sent them flailing into the water. Sailors loading other small boats rushed to rescue them and take them ashore. But the baby was lost. The sailors and some Natives dived in vain to find it. The parents, needless to say, were hysterical with grief, and Reverend Glazier was summoned from the parsonage to comfort them.

Reverend Glazier's two sons pushed off in a rowboat to join the search, and the steamer's captain directed them to tow the overturned skiff, which had drifted some distance away, to shore. When the boys reached the skiff, they turned it right side up so it would be easier to tow. To their amazement, when the skiff flipped over, the baby fell from the bottom side of one of the seats. It had been scooped up when the boat flipped and survived on the seat bottom above the water in air cupped by the inverted hull.

Mrs. Dinniwell's mother, Rachel Glazier, then a small girl, said that to her dying day the most electrifying experience of her life was the sight of the two boys holding the baby aloft. A hush fell, and for a few moments the only sound was that of the baby's cries wafting ashore. Next came pandemonium. The parents shrieked with joy, settlers burst into tears, and Christianized Natives fell to their knees. Reverend Glazier asked everyone to kneel immediately and give thanks for this miracle.

Many years later, in the early 1920s when Mrs. Dinniwell was a young dentist's wife in St. George, she came upon an interesting article on the homemaker's page of Toronto's *Globe and Mail*. It was the story of the baby saved under the seat of the skiff at Cape Croker. The woman writing the piece gave convincing evidence to show that she was indeed that baby. Mrs. Dinniwell regretted never having written to the *Globe and Mail* to get in touch with the woman and perhaps meet her.

The steamer delivering the provisions to the cape that fateful day is thought to be the *J.H. Jones*, a 150-ton wooden supply vessel that sank in a snowstorm off the tip of Cape Croker on November 22, 1906. None of the crew of twelve and nineteen passengers shared the baby's providential good fortune. They all drowned. Only two bodies washed ashore, and the wreck has never been found. The only debris was a small cabin chair plucked from the water by a Native and presented to Mrs. Glazier. She later handed it down to her granddaughter, Mrs. Dinniwell, who in turn gave it to one of her grandchildren residing in Ottawa.

The legends live, but the bits of flotsam stay silent and are treasured for their mysteries.

91

Fearful Reverie

Usually my trips down Memory Lane precede sleep at night, but sometimes a daydream leads me there. One day, now an old man, while basking on a purple Styrofoam noodle on the somnolent Gulf Stream of the John Dolson Pool, I had a fearful reverie. The pool was charitably warm for arthritic seniors, and I drifted over the blue of the deep end far from the gusty flurries sweeping the adjacent schoolyard. Bundled little girls on recess in the yard tapped on the pool window, and I waved to them. Then, closing my eyes, I drifted back sixty-five years.

The urban sprawl around the pool complex, the school, churches, and blocks of apartments dissolved to snow-blown fields of corn stubble lined by oak trees and bramble. I saw Foster's Lane tailing off the end of Lowrey Avenue. Beside the lane, but a couple of hundred yards from where I floated in time, lay a drainage pond. Night fell on my reverie, and I saw my father and a neighbour, Alec Rouse, walking with urgency down the lane. They were carrying hockey sticks, not to play hockey but to probe snowdrifts and pond water for a body.

An alert had gone out over the phone that a little girl had failed to return for supper at Dr. Foster's farm, and the local men had mustered a search. Dr. Foster's farm straddled Moffat Creek at the end of the lane, and the search centred there. But my father and Mr. Rouse got only as far as the drainage pond. There, and I heard him recounting the experience with hushed tones, they came upon several men training dim flashlights on a trail of tiny footprints leading out to a hole in the ice. The men broke the ice and got her out, stiff, blue, and lifeless. There was only three feet of water at the spot, but to her it was bottomless. I believe she was Dr. Foster's granddaughter.

Shock and dread from the little tragedy incited mothers' martial law. For the duration of the winter children could play only within earshot of home after dark. And they could never be late for supper. Every pond became bottomless, and mothers alerted one another about particularly bottomless ponds. The Gooseneck Pond, on a curve of Cheese Factory Road and now part of the Savannah Golf Links, which held barely enough water to float lily pads, became bottomless as soon as it froze over. On the other hand, Oliver's Lake, a quarter mile east of the Gooseneck, really was bottomless.

It was a pond, but because of its depth we called it a lake. No one could find a pole long enough to touch bottom through a hole in the ice in the middle. And rocks lowered on rope descended into the murk until the line, still taut, ran out. The tiny lake and the wooded bog on its south side are today protected by private property, which is fortunate because the area is regarded as an ecological jewel by university biologists. Before it was barred to trespassers we kids skated on it, and people came from miles around to chop holes in the ice to collect in fine mesh nets live feed such as daphne for their aquarium fish. The spring-fed lake water lacked enough oxygen to support fish of its own.

We didn't dare tell our mothers when we were skating on Oliver's Lake. It terrified even us. It was a moody lake. And after a thaw when it shrouded itself in mist so that when you tiptoed to the centre you lost sight of the shore, it became mystical. The ice moaned like a distressed whale and set your hair on end. Then, like a rifle shot, it would crack.

I recall dazzling sunny days on the lake when weekenders with their nets, chatting, drinking, and smoking on folded chairs by the holes they had chopped, leaped to their feet and scampered, arms flapping, for the shore. It was that rifle shot from beneath and the crack, visible to the eye, shooting like lightning. After a few minutes, everyone crept back, but fearfully, hands over their hearts, and the pond would moan, hinting at what it might do again, that it might just part and pull them down into the black.

I miss that scary old wilderness, but in my golden years I have come to prefer the Gulf Stream of the Dolson Pool, the comforting sight of the bottom and, of course, the lifeguards.